POEMS, PATHWAYS AND PEACE

A BABY BOOMER'S JOURNEY WITH ADHD

RON WECKERLY

Outskirts Press, Inc.
Denver, Colorado

Poems, Pathways and Peace
A Baby Boomer's Journey With ADHD
All Rights Reserved.
Copyright © 2010 Ron Weckerly
V6.0 R1.3

Outskirts Press, Inc.
http://www.outskirtspress.com

ISBN: 978-1-59800-544-8

Outskirts Press and the "OP" logo are trademarks belonging to Outskirts Press, Inc.

PRINTED IN THE UNITED STATES OF AMERICA

"The ADHD mind is a rainbow
of colors with gold at the end."

-- Ron Weckerly

Can you imagine there are between eight and ten million adults, maybe more, in the United States walking around not knowing they have ADHD? They may be anxious, impulsive, daydream, and have trouble completing tasks, among other social and psychological problems. Failure, frustration, broken marriages, drug abuse, and loss of jobs are among the major situations that ADHD adults are going through. The ADDer is described as lazy, unmotivated, and unfocused. However, there is a flip side to the adult who has ADD. He or she is usually gifted, intuitive, and full of energy.

In his book, Ron Weckerly shares the extraordinary story of his struggle with ADHD from a very early age through the age of fifty. His journey with ADHD includes failing first grade, having near-death experiences, teachers labeling him as retarded, alcohol abuse, two broken marriages, and feelings of inferiority.

At the age of fifty when he was finally diagnosed with ADHD, he had the "Aha!" experience. Finally knowing that he had ADHD, Ron changed his life for the better. Instead of focusing on his negative traits and disorders, he transformed his weaknesses into strengths. His self-concept improved as well as his overall life skills. His important message is to not wait until the traits become major disorders which ruin your life. Get help as soon as you can if you feel you have ADHD.

Through poetry, Ron shares experiences concerning his challenges with attention-deficit disorder, prose of the fifties and sixties, and short stories that reflect important times in his life. You will discover that Ron's ability to meet the challenges of ADHD helped him to become a successful parent, teacher, and husband.

TABLE OF CONTENTS

ACKNOWLEDGMENTS

I wish to thank the many people who have encouraged me over the years and helped me mature as an individual. To my best friend, Barb Johnson, who died at the age of thirty-five of breast cancer, I say thank you for being my angel on earth; you always stood by me through my various ADHD adventures.

To my daughters, Ginni Weckerly and Heidi Berardi, I express gratitude for loving me for the dad that I was and the new daddy I am today. I called out to you girls many times, and you were always there to understand me and lend support. Your reassuring love and kindness were anchors in the many life storms I have gone through.

I owe much to my wife, Lisa, who loves me and understands my ADHD traits; Lisa is my coach and cheerleader. She rarely gives in to my weaknesses, and builds strengths into our relationship by focusing on my positive points.

I want to give credit to my dogs, Millie, Rosie, and Ruby. They have constantly offered suggestions to me as they lay by my side during the typing of my book; they continuously remind me that love comes in a rainbow of hues; also to Alice, my Springer who has gone on to dog heaven! To my former students, I would like to say thank you for all of your creative talents, understanding, and teaching me many things that I was never taught in college.

Most of all, I want to thank my Lord and Savior, Jesus Christ, who has been with me all the way. God has never given up on me, and I offer my loftiest of praises. If it were not for God, I would not be healed and as healthy as I am today.

INTRODUCTION

As Socrates stated, "An unexamined life is not worth living." I give thanks to Socrates for those words of wisdom. I would be remiss if I did not praise Albert Einstein for one of his many great quotes, "The definition of insanity is doing the same thing over and over again and expecting different results."

By writing my story, I examined and scrutinized my life related to ADHD. The story is not, to a large extent, an autobiography . It is a narrative showing how ADHD greatly influenced the path I traveled. It is amazing what a man discovers about himself when he yearns to share his failures and successes with other people whom he desires to help in life. Wanting to write a book was easier talked about than done! The process has been a painful, yet an enlightening experience; by sharing my life's journey, I have grown stronger and healthier as an individual.

Life is a process of becoming and growing; becoming more self-actualized involves pain, honesty, lonesomeness, frustration, anger, and acceptance. Only when an individual scrutinizes their own life, and is honest in doing so, will they become healthy: physically, mentally, and spiritually. In a nutshell, self-examination and moving forward entail having the guts to see the true self, which I often did not like viewing!

As an ADHD individual, I know what Einstein meant about doing the same thing over and over getting the same results. "I" just did not get it – I cannot tell you how many times I repeated the same negative traits and disorders over and over, getting the same undesirable outcomes!

I believe longing to help others with ADHD by telling my story required me to get out of my "self-pity," and grow as a human. "I am who I am, who people do not think I am."

There is a great future and life beyond ADHD; once I was told that I had the disorder, I was relieved and happy! I finally realized what issues I must take control of and do something about in my life. It was one of those "Aha!" experiences when I found out I had ADHD.

Glancing back to my early life in the 1950s and 1960s, there was no help for an individual as there is today as far as testing, counseling, and medical treatment. I and others my age paid a big price by unknowingly allowing the residual behaviors to grow and become more dominant in our lives. Poor self-esteem, increased depression, anger, and guilt were all elements that attacked my mind, body, and soul.

In my forties I started therapy, which was way too late for dealing with the traits that became major disorders during my life, such as drinking, compulsive behaviors and broken promises. My seemingly harmless traits became disorders and influenced my life greatly in negative ways which not only hurt me, but also the people that I loved.

Once I began psychotherapy, the therapists helped to strike down my tunnel vision of a negative self-image. New avenues of hope were born in becoming a person with self-respect. Talking my problems out was painful, fearful, and exciting at the same time. Old wounds were opened up, yet they were to be healed; the process, however, was hard and challenging.

At the age of fifty, after testing, I became aware that I had ADHD; this was much too long to wait to find out that I had the disorder. The songs of anxieties, rambling thoughts, mood swings, and broken promises spun around in my mind like a record for five long decades. I learned to adapt to some situations; to others, I did not adjust so well.

I became aware bit by bit that drinking and drugs were not the answer to provide temporary calmness to get away from the ADHD symptoms. Acting like a class clown and trying to prove constantly to others that I was good enough were painful and ugly experiences in my life.

I thank God for His guidance and love. He certainly got my attention in the 1980s when He brought me to my knees and I fell before the cross and cried out for His help. I knew I was self-destructing and would kill myself if I continued to treat myself badly. I had to take three months off of work and was in the hospital for over two weeks.

At age sixty-two, I continue to work on my ADHD problems. Having Jesus Christ as my loving Father, I have overcome many negative traits and come to accept my challenges of ADHD. The years of counseling, exercise, and drug therapy have all been good friends in helping me cope with my mayhem. Today, I have modified my diet and that has done wonders!

I would like to invite you, the reader, to come into my world of ADHD:

Come into my world of ADHD, a kaleidoscope of colors.
Gaze at my swirling mind, which is one of a kind.
Listen to my record of thoughts as they spin
     around and around, playing the same old songs.
Come into my world of attention deficit disorder
     and view my creative ideas....
Those concepts that I have thought of and never
     actualized.
The brilliant colors that I possess in my mind's eye,
     assist me in a world that others say is not
          quite correct.
My favorite tones I own are "out of box thinking,"
     a great sense of humor, highly intuitive,
          and persistence in wanting to
               achieve goals.
My positive colors assist me in a world
     that states, "You must conform to
          our world or you are strange."
My darker hues are constantly fighting for
     recognition as my mind floats endlessly
          through space.
The colors of underachievement, mood swings,
     poor tolerance for frustration,
          and sloppy organization,
               are among those attributes
                    that I must color lighter.
The assortment of my light and dark colors
     vie for my attention.

My unfocused mind travels like
        a spinning tornado at times;
These tempestuous colors are lack of remembering,
        impulsivity, a high intense attitude
                and yearning to be a maverick.
Not two ADHD people have the same
        exact tints;
We all play our own 45 rpm of experiences,
        frustrations, disappointments,
                and broken promises.
Our record has two sides…on one face,
        the good attributes of ADHD
                are playing;
On the other side, the challenging qualities
        are spinning around and around.
I urge you to come into my studio of songs
        and pay attention to how
                I have taken my disabilities
                        and turned them into
                                wine from sour grapes.
Hyper-focusing helps me to complete tasks
        in half the time so called "normal" people take.
My ability to read others helps me to be an excellent
        teacher and friend.
The right quadrant of my brain has been good to me.
I can view the entire picture of problems I am studying.
Inside me, at times, I put up a front and really
        do not recognize the person that I am
                pretending to be.
I yearn to be human; nothing
        more and nothing less.
As I saunter and run life's peaks and valleys,
I will never be that person who goes with the "flow"
        and who is perfect in the eyes of others or
                myself.
I am the artist of my life;
I embrace my palette of colors
        and continue to work on my self-portrait.
I continue to search for the various ways

I may combine my light and dark colors
to allow myself to grow and
become a better human.
Move toward my world, I invite you again.
Like you, I cry, hurt, am happy, have future plans,
and want others to have a good life.
In the end, you will discover, that we are
more alike than different.
Come into my world...
There I go again...
Saying things over and over!

CHAPTER ONE

THE EARLY YEARS

I was born on August 18, 1947 in St. Francis Hospital to Vernon and Betty Weckerly. Like most parents, my mom and dad were proud to have a big, bouncing baby boy -- over nine pounds! I had brown curly hair and sky blue eyes like my mother's. To add to my charm, I had a big head, and people thought that I might be retarded and have a physical deformity!

I lived my first five years on Miami Street in Freeport, Illinois. My father was a blue-collar worker who drove a taxi and a truck for all of his working life. My mother did not work, and stayed at home until I was around ten years old. Then, Mom got a job at Firestone Tire Company and later worked at Micro Switch, a factory, in Freeport on Stevenson Street. Dad did not graduate from high school; he had a sixth-grade education. The story goes that he got into all kinds of trouble in junior high. Dad did not study; he got into fights and caused problems for his parents. The principal called Dad's parents and told them they needed to talk about Vernon's behavior. Well, his parents decided he would be better off quitting school and earning money; they never went in and had a conference, and that was the end of Dad's school career. Dad was a rough, tall, and lean man around six feet four inches. He was a hard worker and a no-nonsense type of man.

Looking back, Dad was a great example of a person who had ADHD. He was impulsive, had a bad temper, drank to medicate himself, made promises and did not keep them, and suffered from depression. Back in the 1930s, no one had a clue about the characteristics of ADHD and how to diagnose its traits. I am sure if Dad could have had medication and therapy, his life would have been much different. The consequences of ADHD will continue into generations if not corrected and dealt with when recognized, as seen in my family.

Mother was loving and supportive, yet she did not know what was going on with her son, Ron. Whenever I was going through major issues as a child and adult, Mom reassured me things would get better. She possessed a strong faith in Jesus Christ. She was correct; things always turned out for the better.

My sister, Sherry, was three years older than I; we got along like most brothers and sisters. We fought at times and played well at times. Sherry was very smart and performed well in school. I was the slow learner who struggled in the academics. I was good in sports, which helped get me through my ADHD issues for a certain length of time. Looking back, I feel sorry that my sister had to put up with my anxiety issues and temper tantrums, which influenced our relationship as brother and sister. After graduating from high school, my sister was accepted to Michael Reese Hospital in Chicago, Illinois; we did not have the opportunity to see each other on a daily basis after she went off to nursing school. This affected our relationship, as I did not get to share a lot about myself with Sherry in the important years of my life due to the geographic distance between us.

As I mentioned, I was a jock and Sherry was into studying and school. I was popular with peers, and my sister was more into academics than the social realm. My strength of intra- and inter-personal traits were saving graces as I advanced in my school years, but academics did not do any favors as far as enhancing friendships.

The year was 1954, and I was starting kindergarten at Center School, which was only two blocks from where I lived. Dwight D. Eisenhower was president, Dr. Jonas Salk announced his discovery of the polio vaccine, and Peter Pan proudly premiered on the American scene. This year, too, I was starting my journey in life with the American educational system.

Attending kindergarten was exciting, yet I did not know, like most of the children my age, what to expect the first day. Besides the normal fears and concerns, this day was not all that horrible. I brought my rug to sleep on and other supplies to put into those small cubicles or lockers. I was introduced to the teacher and other students. It was the days, months, and years that followed that would be challenging for me. It was normal to put your shoes on backwards, not to button your raincoat correctly, and to reverse "b" and "d" occasionally. I was one of those students who frequently emitted the inappropriate behaviors, as well as not knowing what to do academically and behaviorally to be a success. However, one must consider the frequency, intensity, and duration of behaviors to see if there are problems academically or behaviorally.

I was victorious and made it through Kindergarten ok -- it was in the 1954-1955 school year when I started first grade that my academic and social problems would stand out from those of my peers.

In 1954, the US Supreme Court ruled against racial segregation in schools, and the World Series was broadcast in color for the first time. Little did I realize that having ADHD was going to segregate me all my life into lower classes. I would be labeled lazy, and one who did not try in academics. Like the World Series, my true colors of a child with learning problems began to show for the first time.

My teacher, Mrs. Putman, gave the class directions on how to do a math problem; I immediately forget what she told us. I would be peering out the window counting the birds instead of focusing on math. It seemed that from a very early age, I had my "own way" of thinking on how to do math and reading. Another issue…I forgot to bring items to school on a daily basis. My organizational skills were poor; in fact, I think I did not have any! I rushed out the door to go to school and forgot my homework, pencils, and crayons. After school, I repeated the same process, never thinking of what to bring home. My mind was swirling and spinning around like a whirlwind. The constant forgetting only fostered embarrassment and started to damage my self-esteem at a young age.

Perhaps my major problem was focusing and paying attention: my short term memory skills were terrible. How could I remember anything when my mind was racing around like a 45 rpm record?

As far as reading, I had trouble with pronouncing words and understanding the context of the words in a sentence. We learned by the sight word method. Phonetics were not taught as they are today in the schools. To this day, at age sixty-two, I still have trouble with pronouncing words; I give thanks to spell check and the dictionary for helping me out!

My peers laughed at me when I tried to read. This only encouraged me to not want to read in front of others. I peered into their laughing faces after I did not read a word correctly, feeling terrible. This image followed me into high school and beyond. Ironically, I felt that I was smart and I could read as well as others, but just did not know how to go about doing so.

At the end of the school year in 1955, Mrs. Putnam called my mother and me to school for a conference - a meeting that I recall vividly today. Mrs. Putnam and my mom asked me what I thought about being held back to improve my reading skills. My mother asked me, "Ronnie, what do you think about being retained since you cannot read and remember things well?" What could I do but agree with Mom and Mrs. Putnam? At that very moment, I felt empty, frustrated, and embarrassed. The next school year would be telling, regarding how I was developing as a student.

The school year was 1955-1956 and history was moving forward. Dr. Martin Luther King Jr. led his first major civil rights event in Montgomery, Alabama concerning school busing, President Eisenhower had a heart attack, and Ron Weckerly was to be challenged in different ways in repeating first grade.

Entering first grade again made me feel like a big fish out of water. I was doing better in reading and math, so the philosophy of holding me back helped academically. However, socially, I felt humiliated and different than most of my friends. I was bigger, stronger, and possessed a different way of thinking than most of the "normal" kids.

My gross motor skills, reading, and math skills were average, and I tried with all my heart to keep up with those that were so much better than I was academically. Socially, the students liked me, but I knew they were thinking about how I was held back. Frequently on the playground, I excelled in playing sports; the students would say to me that I was good because I was held back a year in school. Comments like this only reinforced the idea that I was a loser and never could live up to the expectations of others.

Soon the summer of 1956 was starting, and I made it through first grade -- not, however, without scars and hurts I wanted to heal. I enjoyed the summers between the school years. They gave me time to just be a kid and not worry about academics, peer pressure, and how I could catch up to others and be in the "smart" classes. When I went to elementary school, the administration segregated the smart kids and the slow learners. I was always in the slow classes. This only added to my inferiority complex -- I would never be with my friends who were more intelligent.

In the summer, we played and I expelled some of the pent-up energy which was toxic in my mind and body. We played kick the can, red light, and other fun games. However, the hood kids made make fun of me even though we were not in school. ADHD is like a snowball rolling down a hill: the problems only get worse if the disorder is not diagnosed and dealt with professionally. My traits of depression, a poor self-concept, anxiety, and temper tantrums would become major disorders later in my life.

During the summer of 1956, I went to the hospital to get my tonsils taken out. I recall my mother calling me into the kitchen and sharing with me that I had to have the operation. Dr. Becker, my physician, would take them out. We would be going to St. Francis Hospital in Freeport to have the operation. Like most children, I was afraid and skeptical about the whole process. Mom, again, told me I should trust the Lord, and things would turn out fine.

On Monday, I went to St. Francis and had what was considered to be minor surgery in the 1950s. To this day I can smell the ether that was given to me during the operation! The surgery went fine and I was taken to a hospital room for recovery. It is while I was in recovery that a major event of my life happened. The nurse, who was a nun, gave me a piece of hard toast after the operation. This tore open my stitches that the doctor sewed up. I started throwing up blood; I sat up in my bed and cupped my hands as the blood filled my hands like an overflowing volcano.

The next thing I was aware of was swirling through a gray and white tunnel. I was moving rather fast; at the end of the tunnel, I saw an angel-like figure reaching out her hands to assist me through the end of the passageway. She had rosy pink cheeks and golden hair. Just as I was about to be helped out of the end of the tunnel into the angel's arms, I regained consciousness. As my eyes roamed the walls, I noticed a crucifix hanging beside my bed on the wall. It was as if Christ was hovering over me and watching all the events of the evening taking place.

Awaking, I heard the doctor ask the nurse, "What the hell were you thinking?" I recall this remark clearly. The doctor told my mother that I had no heartbeat for three minutes. To this day, I still wonder whether the incident added to my ADHD, or caused it to be more severe.

I was getting ready for third grade, which was the 1956-1957 school year. Mrs. Benson would be my new teacher for the upcoming year. She was tall, had rounded glasses, a jutted jaw, and beautiful brown eyes. Her smile was as warm as the sun on a hot summer day.

Mrs. Benson, I thought, understood me more than the other teachers I had previously. She asked me to come in at recess and work on my math and reading skills. She was patient and repeated things to me that I did not understand. My self-image was improving slightly by third grade; however, I still possessed my undesirable skills of not paying attention, interrupting people, and being disorganized. I recall third grade as a year of improvement as far as someone caring for the direction I was heading. I started to get Cs and Bs in spelling, reading, and math.

Soon third grade passed, and I had the summer of 1957 to enjoy with my friends and family. I enjoyed playing in the "hood," although my so-called friends teased me about my big water head and stupid brain. As an ADDer, I wanted badly to be accepted by others. There were two boys next door who were several years older than me. I yearned to become accepted by them and be their friends. Their names were Pat and Mike. They told me I could be their friend if I would do certain things to earn their friendships.

One time, they asked me to call a lady a bad name. I hid behind the bushes and yelled out, "You bitch!" I then ran down the street and hid where no one could see me. Both Pat and Mike laughed and laughed. I probably laughed too, but what a price to pay for friendship. I ended up playing basketball and baseball with the boys quite frequently this summer of 1957.

I enjoyed playing with my dog Blackie, and going to stock car races out at Freeport Speedway during the summers. I told Blackie all of my problems; I felt she understood me more than some people. It was like Blackie was my saving grace. I enjoyed her licking my face in acknowledgment of sharing my troubles with her. Freeport Speedway was fun, as I would go out and watch the racers zoom around the half mile dirt track. The hot dogs tasted wonderful and the dirt that landed in my coke from the speeding cars' dust added to the flavor of the summer evenings.

Next to my old home on Miami Street stood Joe's Grocery Store, where my parents shopped. I got up early in the summer mornings and watched the delivery trucks bring their goods to the store. It was fun watching the Wonder Bread trucks deliver bread and pastries to Joe's Store. The delivery man, who unloaded his goods at the store, was always pleasant to me. I continually asked him if he had any extra Hostess Cupcakes or Twinkies. I was lucky a couple times, as he gave me some extras; he probably thought, "I should get this kid off my back by giving him some samples!" The sugar that I was eating only contributed to my ADHD symptoms of hyperactivity and depression, but it tasted great!

During the summer of 1957, I went fishing with my dad in some of the creeks around Freeport. It was one of my favorite things to do with dad. We hunted for worms the night before and put them in an old coffee can for our trip to the creek the following day. I hooked pan fish and turtles in the creeks we fished. Once I caught a big snapping turtle; we took it home and put it in my grandpa's garage. The next day when I got up to see the turtle, it was gone! Grandpa told me that it probably crawled to a sewer to get water. I think he made it into turtle soup and did not want to tell about the demise of the reptile! I started to go to church during the summer of 1957. My parents did not go with me; they would drop my sister and me off at church and pick us up after the services. This bothered me greatly, as I yearned to worship with my family. It hurt to see other families going to church together and enjoying the fellowship. At a very young age, I felt a calling to go into the ministry; I believe this was partly to do with almost dying from my tonsils being taken out, and my religious up-bringing from my mother's mom.

The summer of 1957 swiftly passed, and it was time to go into fourth grade. I cannot recall who my teacher was this year, but I continued to work hard to cover up my disorders of ADHD and my learning disabilities. It was still difficult for me to sit still, concentrate, recall information, and to stop my racing mind in the classroom and at home

During the school years 1958 and 1959, the Soviet Union launched Sputnik I; the movie *Bridge on the River Kwai* made its debut; and the TV show *Perry Mason* came on the scene. In addition, the famous Slinky and Hula Hoop were introduced to our childhood toys.

During fourth grade, I overheard my parents talking about how the teachers felt that I might be retarded! I scored only 100 on the Stanford-Binet and my mind was moving at a snail's pace in academics. At a very early age I was labeled as a "slow learner." I carried this label with me going from year to year in my schooling. During the fourth grade I continued to work on my basic facts and reading skills. I now added OCD (obsessive compulsive disorder) to my list of behavior problems. Whenever I touched papers, I did not want to throw the papers away because my fingerprints were on the them. I would think that I was throwing a part of myself away when I tossed paper into a wastebasket. The OCD disorder is characterized by a recurrent and intrusive kind of thinking. This thinking could be about counting, washing your hands continually, or repeating words and phrases over and over in your mind. My OCD feelings about my fingerprints were constantly playing on my mind's swirling 45 rpm record. These invasive thoughts stopped me from learning and hurt my emotional health. How could I get the information being presented when my mind was not focused on what was being taught? Today, researches have discovered that people who have ADHD and OCD may have problems in the orbit frontal cortex of the brain.

In the fourth grade, I was getting Bs and Cs and maintaining my skills, but had a hard time learning new skills. In the classroom my organizational skills were not improving. My desk looked like a "garbage heap," as it was cluttered with paper, pencils, and glue. I recall that the glue used to spill out and get all over my papers, causing a real mess! My worrying became more toxic in the fourth grade. I constantly wanted to be accepted by my peers. I worried about my parents, sister, and other things which I had no control over.

In December of 1958, I almost lost my life due to the anxiety I was dealing with. I had the tendency to eat quickly and not take my time. While at Thanksgiving dinner, I was eating dry turkey and started choking. My family called the ambulance -- however, my cousin Hoby did first aid on me and dislodged the turkey. Again, ADHD was to blame: the anxiety and hurried behavior I exhibited almost cost me my life once again!

During fourth grade, my parents realized that I needed extra help with my homework. Whenever Mother tried to help me, I would get frustrated. Perhaps, I could feel her frustration with my inability to learn and pick up concepts at a fast pace. Mom hired a tutor to help with my spelling and reading. She asked Mrs. Doering, the principal's wife, to tutor me. Dad and Mom could scarcely afford the five bucks Mrs. D charged per hour, but thought I would benefit from the extra coaching.

I recall Mrs. Doering giving me a break from studying -- we watched *"To Tell the Truth"* on TV. She awarded me a treat, and after I ate the candy we continued practicing spelling words; this may be where I got my behavior modification techniques, and not from the college subjects that I took!

Overall, the fourth grade went well, and I survived. Reflecting back to my early years, I knew when I was constantly stimulated, felt excitement, and could be creative, I was at my best as a learner. Rote memorization did not do it for me academically, and today, I still have the desire to learn in many different ways.

In the 1959-1960 school year, I entered the fifth grade. The summer of 1959 went well and I was looking forward to fifth grade. This year I had Mr. Moen, a teacher, who expected a lot from us. He was demanding, yet a fair teacher who cared about each of his students. He was a traditional, no-nonsense type of teacher; if you did not pay attention, you might get an eraser thrown at you to redirect your mind! More than one day, I went home with chalk dust along the side of my head.

Mr. Moen gave us more homework in the fifth grade. I did not possess any study skills, so I really did not know how to go about learning and completing assigned work. My frustration increased because of my emotional issues. I became aggravated at the slightest noises at home, did sloppy work, and pouted when I just did not get the information I needed to learn.

Back in the 1950s we were not aware that there were professionals such as educational psychologists, social workers, and doctors who could give medication to help you concentrate. We never heard them mentioned at school or at home. For the most part, we had to survive on our own and learn the best way that we knew how. The word "survivor" is a name that I have carried on my shoulders as an ADHDer all of my life.

In the summer of 1959, I continued to play baseball, which I loved to do. I was twelve years old and enjoyed doing something that was fun and entertaining. In 1959, I made the all-star team and played first base part of the time. It was a fun and exhilarating experience for a young man who was used to failure and frustrations in school.

I want to flashback and share with you an ADHD incident which happened in 1957. I was nine years old and I wanted to try out for Little League baseball. I was hyperactive as a kid; I bothered and teased my sister to the point where I made her cry. One humid and hot summer day, my sister refused to allow me to play with her and a friend. Sherry locked me out of the house and I became angry. I lost my temper and flew off the handle; I tried to push up the window and crawl into the house. Instead, I pushed through the window and shattered the glass. The sharp glass cut my wrist and just missed an artery. My friends, the Milligan boys, and their dad, Carl, took me to the hospital; this delayed my entry into Little League baseball. However, I recovered and got to play when I was ten years old.

I was entering the sixth grade in 1960. The teacher I had this year was Mrs. Eckhart, who had a great impact on me for the rest of my life. For some reason, Mrs. Eckhart understood what I was going through internally as an individual. She encouraged me to do my homework and stay on task, and tried to keep me actively involved in the discussions that were taking place in class. Mrs. Eckhart appeared again later in my life when I won an award as a teacher.

With Mrs. Eckhart, I was allowed to be innovative and she frequently changed her pace in teaching. She not only taught individual activities, but group projects. In sixth grade, I felt better about the person I was becoming. The next school year, 1961-1962 was going to be exciting and fun, yet very challenging for me academically and socially.

Going on to seventh grade was a new ballgame altogether from elementary school. I would be meeting new friends, trying out for sports, and being introduced to new teaching styles. I still had the desire to be in the "smart kid" classes, and be recognized for being talented.

My poor elementary school records and IQ followed me like a dark shadow and did no favors for me. While many of my elementary school friends were in the advanced classes, I was in the low average classes. I continued struggling in reading, math, science, and social studies as these subjects concerned word recognition and comprehension skills as well as writing mechanics. My best subject was PE class; I was a straight A student in the physical realm. I am sure my pent-up anxiety helped me to excel.

One symptom of ADHD, my hyperactivity, changed in my adolescent years. My anxiety and constant physical motion were lessened because of my involvement in sports. I played football, basketball, and ran track during my middle school years. I burned up a lot of energy participating in the various sports and working out every day.

Another area that was undergoing transformation was my ability to focus during class. Because of exercise, my mind was now clearer and I could understand more of what the teacher was saying. The exercise was like medication for me. Today, psychiatrists and psychologists say that exercising is a natural medication for living a better life with ADHD.

In seventh grade, I was liked by the other students because of my involvement in sports. During the first semester of my seventh grade year, I was interviewed for the *Green Banner,* the seventh grade newspaper. I found that to be a very motivating and a positive thing in my academic career. The writers asked me about my ambitions, family, and goals in life. This was the first time I got positive recognition from my peers, and I felt accepted.

During my seventh grade school year, 1960-1961, a lot was occurring in history. John F. Kennedy was entering his first term as President of the United States, Cassius Clay won his first professional fight, and soldiers were on their way to Vietnam. One of Clay's famous statements was, "I am the greatest." Along with Joe Lewis, Clay was one of the greatest fighters of all time. In contrast, I felt that I was far from being the greatest, and, internally, I was losing out on life in many ways. I was still struggling with poor organizational skills, toxic worrying, a foggy mind, and a poor self-concept.

On the positive side, as I mentioned, I was doing well in sports in seventh grade. I started on the basketball team and football teams. Again, sports boosted my confidence, and some of that transferred over into my academics. My gift of intuition helped me in reading people and getting along with them. In addition, my ADHD quality of being zany and fun helped me when I was with my peers in social settings. My deep compassion for people assisted me in understanding them. Ironically, my lost self also helped me in being sensitive with other students who were struggling with personal problems; a gift of empathy is not all bad!

I continued to work on my memory and study skills. Processing information was very difficult. It was like hammering and pounding information over and over into my brain until it registered; it was painful. However, I discovered once the information was registered in my brain, my long term memory skills were great. I continued to invent my own unique ways of studying to become a better student. I placed vocabulary words on note cards and selected colors in note-taking to assist my recall. I used my favorite colors and symbols in learning important points. During seventh grade, I continued to get Cs and Bs; I never made the honor roll, which I so desperately wanted to do. However, I had one great teacher who touched my life. His name was Mr. Wells, my math teacher. He took the time and energy to ask me to come in after school and work on my fractions and percentages. Math involves abstract thinking, which I did not possess. Mr. Wells taught me with diagrams and colors to help convert fractions to percentages. I felt Mr. Wells introduced me to a special learning style which I use today: visual- memory skills.

I passed the seventh grade without any major problems and soon entered the eighth grade for the 1961-1962 school year. The seventh grade was good to me, as far as maintaining my grades and grow-ing as an individual. However, I still possessed ADHD traits, which were contradictory tendencies swirling around in my mind and soul like mini-tornadoes. I was happy one moment, sad the next, and un-predictable in my behavior toward others and very impulsive.

A few of the historical events taking place in 1961 were: President Kennedy established the Peace Corps; the Soviet Union built the wall between East and West Berlin, and the "Freedom Riders" traveled to the South to promote integration. They were beaten and assaulted in trying to promote the Civil Rights Movement. I was moving forward trying to find freedom in my soul and heart and understand how I too was so different from my peers. I yearned to have free thinking and feel alive like my peers.

Eighth grade went well for me as I continued to hold my own socially and academically. I sustained my place in sports, tried to learn my best, and felt that I was moving forward. I spoke to some of my smarter friends and tried to learn how they studied. Many offered suggestions on their study habits and how to do homework --like being organized, breaking work down into smaller segments and not waiting until the last minute to do homework.

I continued to worry about the "ifs" in my life: wondering if my fellow students liked me, wondering if my parents would get a divorce...the "ifs" were wearing me down emotionally. I had the tendency to repeat the same mistakes over and over without trying to correct myself. For example, I made promises to my friends, and then broke those agreements. I wanted to please people so badly that I went along with them even if I did not really desire to do so in the first place.

The academic year went by quickly, and the summer of 1962 was soon at my door. I played Babe Ruth baseball, went swimming, and did little during the summer to improve my academics. It was important that I continue to read and write during the summer; how-ever, I did not participate in any academic programs at the library. Summer learning would have helped me a great deal; however, I chose not to attend any of the reading programs, which was a major mistake.

The school year of 1962-1963 was overflowing with challenges and frustrations. I like to point out, we all have challenges and frustrations in life; however, the ADHD person compounds these challenges because he or she has chemical disorders. Our minds fire off like ping pong balls being hit back and forth on a table.

During ninth grade the vexations of trying to keep up with my peers academically continued in my mind. My peers were taking foreign languages and algebra. I was not in a foreign language class -- I was having trouble with English; how could I do well in a second language? In my heart, I felt like I could do that work; I sensed that I was being cheated out of an education.

My parents reluctantly signed a note and gave counselors permission for me to try a foreign language. Well, I had much difficulty, as the language required memorization and English skills. In addition, I had auditory-discrimination problems and had trouble hearing and speaking the language. I was desperate, so I cheated on a test. I got caught and was almost kicked off the basketball team. It was an embarrassing moment for me in front of my peers and teachers. I went back to my French teacher and apologized for my behavior. I did not have the confidence to learn. I continued to be labeled as "lazy" and as an underachiever in my academics and life, especially after this incident of cheating.

We had a great basketball team in ninth grade. We went 29-1; we played as a team and expected a lot from each other. I felt accepted on the basketball court. I was good and could score points and be recognized not only by my peers but by teachers as well. My mood disorders continued to be a fight for me. I could not understand the "elevator" that I was on. One moment I was high, the next moment I was low and depressed; if only I could think clearly and not have a cloudy and moody mind. On the positive side, I was tenacious and persistent in wanting to change and become a better person. Yet the yearning to do better was an overwhelming task. How could I change if I did not know exactly how to modify my behaviors?

During the summer of 1963, a significant event happened in my life. My Grandpa Roy died. Grandpa was a powerful figure in my life. Whenever Dad was not around to take me to my baseball games, Grandpa would be there for a ride. Grandpa had a strong belief in Jesus Christ and we frequently talked about the Lord and what He could do in our lives. The loss of my grandpa seemed to help reshape me in some ways. I knew that life is always changing and that a strong person must learn to blow with life's winds and adjust their own sails. I knew that change was possible, but difficult, and it took work and discipline to modify one's behavior.

An event happened which almost took my life during July of 1963. I went to Kansas to visit my cousin, Gary. Gary was like a brother that I never had; we got along well and loved each other. My uncle Don asked me if I'd like to come out for a couple weeks. My parents allowed me to go and see Sandy and Gary. I ended up staying around six weeks, to the displeasure of my mom and dad.

One hot summer day, my cousins and I went swimming in a lake near where they lived. This is where my impulsivity came out in a big way. I was showing off to my cousins and a nice-looking girl. I wanted to prove to them that I could swim out to the warning ropes in the lake. I dove into the water and off I went, about to create my own demise. As I was splashing and swimming toward the boundaries of the no-swim area, I lost all my strength. I called out to my cousin Sandy; she saw me in desperation and yelled for the lifeguard. Thank God, he swam out and grabbed me just in time--I was going down deep into the water and would not come up again. His strong arms embraced my limp body and saved my life.

So often, I gave no thought to the stupid things I did without considering the consequences. That night, I could not sleep and had the night sweats; my aunt, Dot, was kind and gentle in helping me overcome my emotional experience, and stayed up most of the night with me.

In August of 1963, I returned home in one piece physically, but emotionally, I was not well. I was going to start tenth grade with my backpack of depression, anger, inattention, impulsivity, poor self-esteem, and disorganization. My increasingly aggressive behavior was not good and would be a major issue for not only my sophomore year in high school, but all of my life.

I started off the school year by playing football. We met in the heat of August to practice and get ready for the first game in September 1963. During August, I turned sixteen and was eligible for my driver's license. I was the first kid to take the driver's exam, because of the fact that I was held back in first grade. I felt awkward about having the honor to be the initial student tested for a driver's license. The idea that I was the first of my peers to do so made me feel honored, yet labeled. I knew in my heart that others were saying, "Weck is first because he failed a grade."

The coaches gave me permission to skip practice and go for my driver's exam. All eyes were upon Weck; I would be the first in my class to drive a car. Off I went to the driver's station in hopeful anticipation of getting the valued certificate. You guessed it right -- I failed the test and, again, being a failure was reinforced. My friends could not believe that I failed to pass a simple exam. I passed the written exam, but not the driving part! It was later in October when I retook the test and passed it. The first time, I forgot to turn the wheels into the curb when downhill parking. The second time, I passed with flying colors.

I played left tackle in football my sophomore year. I performed well and was excited, looking forward to basketball season. Football was not my favorite sport; it was basketball and baseball. During one of the games against East High School, I cracked my wrist while trying to make an open field tackle; the end result was that I started basketball season late.

My sophomore year of high school was both good and bad. I played well in basketball and was improving academically. However, this year is when my ADHD traits were becoming disorders. The major issue was my anxiety; to feel better, I started drinking.

Politics were great in Freeport; they played a major role if you played sports. During my sophomore year, the coach wanted to play everyone. He especially wanted to play those who were heading toward college and a promising life. I was not one of those. I recall going to my sophomore basketball coach and asking him why I was not playing full time. He could not explain himself. My numbers were very good in scoring points and rebounding; however, that was not good enough in his eyes!

My dad, whom I loved very much, was not doing me any favors. He came to the games drunk and yelled at the coaches and refs. This was doing more harm than good. I also had a temper that caused me problems. I flew off the handle at times during practice and would get into fights with my teammates.

I would like to share with you an example of what an ADHD person can do concerning hyper-focusing; this was an experience I had while playing basketball my sophomore year. Toward the end of the year, I was placed on second string. I knew I should be playing first string. The coach told us in scrimmage that the team who won could start against LaSalle-Peru. The agreement was that the first string would replace the second team when we started to get behind. Guess what? We never got behind the other team! I scored a high of thirty-three points that game! It was not quite a school record -- I missed it by six points. The coach came to me in the fourth quarter and asked if he could put in a replacement. I told him that he could; however, he never substituted for me.

On November 23, at 12:30 P.M. my life and the lives of others were about to change forever. President John F. Kennedy was assassinated. We were getting out of swimming class and one of our teachers, Mr. Smith, came reeling around the corner. He yelled, "President Kennedy has been assassinated." To this day, I vividly recall how we reacted with disbelief, sorrow, and anger. Later in the day, we gathered at a student's house to view the media coverage. We cried and talked about the horrible event. I feel that world history would have been quite different if JFK had been around for the full presidency.

The rest of the 1963-1964 school year went well, but my problems with drinking and not feeling accepted by my peers and the coaches continued. In the spring, I tried out for baseball, but was placed on the JV team. I knew I could have played varsity, but I felt my behavior and politics hurt me again.

During the summer of 1964, I worked at a local factory, Burgess Battery, and played baseball. It was fun during the summer, but I knew my junior and senior years would be trouble concerning sports. I continued to hang around the wrong crowd, and my drinking tribulations only compounded my ADHD issues. The fall would come soon, along with more personal issues as I started my junior year of high school.

During my junior year my anxiety became worse, and the one thing which made me a better person -- sports -- was no longer going to help me with my peers and teachers. With ADHD, anxiety disorders are frequently found. In fact, most adults who have grown up with undiagnosed ADHD have a mild case of PTSD (Post-Traumatic Stress Disorder). The reason is that untreated ADHD leads to episodes of humiliation, failure, rejection, and trauma. By the time I was in high school, letdown after letdown was being realized. I established goals, and not many were actualized because of the undiagnosed ADHD and depression.

My junior year I played junior varsity football and was really unhappy with the situation, although it was fun. I was looking forward to my senior year playing varsity ball. However, that never happened. My coach, who promised me during the summer of 1965 that I would play in the fall, cut me from the team; I even went to his house and practiced with him!

To add to my stress, my junior year, I was cut from the basketball team. How it happened was very humiliating. During practice before the season, the coaches played certain players in exhibition games. I was the last one to be asked to participate in the scrimmages. I then knew I was going to be cut from the team. To this day, I ask myself why the coaches didn't tell me not to come out for the varsity team. I believe it was for a variety of reasons. As I stated before, I had temper issues and drinking problems. By cussing at the refs and coaches, my dad did not do much to help me out. In addition, my dad was not high class in the Freeport community; and I was not supposed to go to college, in the eyes of the community and teachers.

During my junior and senior years, my sports activities declined, and I experienced extreme anxiety and depression. As a senior, I started at first base in baseball, but I did not do my best. The boozing and depression were making me unhealthy; I was not focusing on school or playing sports.

I hung around drinkers my senior year; my former friends, who were jocks, went their way and I went mine. Many of my so-called friends were heading to private colleges and universities, and I was staying in Freeport to try to get into a junior college.

With my undiagnosed ADHD, I was doing everything I should not be doing: consuming an improper diet with too much sugar and carbohydrates, drinking alcohol, not exercising, and not getting enough rest.

After graduating from high school in 1966, despite my fight with ADHD vexations of a foggy mind, anxiety, and depression, I coped the best way I knew at the time; I was in a deep state of denial about my social and behavioral issues.

CHAPTER TWO

COLLEGE AND BEYOND

In the fall of 1966, I started attending Highland Community College in Freeport, Illinois, my home town. Highland was just getting started as a junior college. I was lucky because the college was probably desperate for students. In order to get into Highland, I had to take English 099. It was a remedial English course for those of us who did not know the English language well. There was a whopping total of six students in Mr. Spudich's class. I was fortunate to have a man that cared for his students and wanted them to be successful in college and in life.

Mr. Spudich used sentence diagramming to help us understand the relationships among nouns, verbs, and adjectives in sentences; I have to smile, as I used this method for my sixth grade students many years later. I learned a lot about sentence and paragraph structure from Mr. Spudich. I passed remedial English and later took English 100, a freshamn course, that was required.

During my freshman year at Highland, I was elected vice president of the student body. My gift of possessing a good personality helped me to get elected. The students liked me for the crazy and zany person that I was. During my first semester at Highland, I got a 2.5 average -- not bad for someone who started college without many study skills. I was studying more; I really wanted to go to Carthage College. As I stated earlier, my dream from a very young age was to go into the ministry.

Another professor I had at Highland College was Mr. Peace. He taught Educational Psychology. Mr. Peace assisted me in learning how to study. I told him that I never learned the correct study skills. He shared with me how to distribute my studying over time and break it down into small pieces. He said that many students waited until the last minute and mass practiced. This method helped out tremendously -- if I studied a little each day, I did not feel overwhelmed.

During my freshman year at Highland, I again almost died because of my hurried pace. I ate dinner quickly, which consisted of only an apple. I needed to get to choir practice on time at Professor Grey's house. I ate and went to class. While singing, I started to choke. I pointed to my chest and the professor laid me on the floor and whacked my back. I could feel the apple fall from my diaphragm. I have Professor Grey to thank for his quick action. So again, this was the fourth time I almost lost my life! Post-traumatic stress disorder was becoming part of my ADHD profile.

I applied to Carthage College in Kenosha, Wisconsin. I received a 4-D deferment from the government, which meant I was going into divinity school. The year I entered Carthage was 1968, and I was happy to be going off to school. If I had been a rational person, I should have stayed at Highland for another year. My drinking, depression, anxiety, and lack of confidence were elements that I was denying. I needed to become mentally healthy, but I did not know I was sick. To change a behavior, you must realize that you have certain disorders and deal with them. Denial was a great friend in my early years of college and beyond.

When starting my first year at Carthage, I wanted to be accepted by others. If this meant drinking and acting like a clown, I would do what was necessary to be accepted. Many of us ADDers are attracted to others who have the same issues. We enjoy hanging around risk takers, drinkers, and people who are not good role models. If you asked how many people I went out with in college whom I truly respected, I would say, "Not one!" I prized them only because they had negative traits like I possessed! That made it easy not to look critically at myself and make the positive changes I needed to make; it also helped me to continue in denial!

During the first semester at Carthage, I cannot recall ever opening a book and studying. My disorder was completely out of control. My anxiety skyrocketed, and my self-esteem was elevated only by drinking. The first semester I got Ds and Fs at Carthage. Going into the spring semester of 1968, things did not change. I drank and squandered any money that I possessed. I continued to associate with people who were not good role models for me. I have to admit that I was not good for the people I hung around with during my stint at Carthage, either. I was associating with students who would put me down in different ways if I did not do what they wanted me to do. I longed badly to have people love me for the individual that they really did not know; the person inside of me who loves, cares, and yearns to celebrate life.

My risky behaviors continued while at Carthage. I would get drunk and hang on the back of cars and be pulled around in the snowy streets. I am one lucky guy to have survived the ordeals that I put myself through. I went drinking and ended up almost getting into fights at bars. I was spending money on booze that I should have been saving for my education. I had no regard for my parents, who worked hard to send me to Carthage.

About thirty of us students had a party while at Carthage College. We were all jammed into a tiny motel room. Some of the students who attended the merrymaking drove across the motel's lawn and damaged the grass. The owner showed up at the door with a pistol in his hand; he demanded we pay for the damage of the lawn. The proprietor told us to write down our names and where we lived -- most of the students listed false names and addresses. I, however, put down my real name and address. We all left the party scared to death. I collected around $200 to pay for the damages. Two days later I got a call from the manager of the hotel; he wanted to talk to me. I was scared, but went to meet and apologize again for our behavior. He gave back the $200. This incident was an example of risky and inappropriate behaviors that evolved from my ADHD, a disorder which I did not know I possessed. Not knowing that I had ADHD was not an excuse for my behavior, but perhaps helps explain why I exhibited some of the bizarre behaviors.

Insecurity and dishonesty were residuals of ADHD that were growing every day since my youth. My ugly duckling self-concept was being reinforced daily by the negative behaviors I exhibited. As I mentioned, all I wanted was someone to see there was good in me -- that I was not a flake, but a person of value. Since I was a child, I wanted someone to say, "Hey Weck, I like you for being a kind and gentle person." However, by the time you get to be an adult with undiscovered ADHD, it is hard to seek out those people who will see the positive traits in you. As far as dishonesty, I cheated on a Philosophy of Religion paper. I was caught and given an F by the professor. Can you imagine there are millions of adults in the United States walking around not knowing they have ADHD? I can laugh at that now, but it was not a laughing matter at the time!

While at Carthage in the spring of 1968, a major historical event occurred. Dr. Martin Luther King was shot to death on April 4th. I recall playing pool in the union with my two friends, Ike and Howard. A news flash came on TV that King had been shot. The three of us went back to the dorms and smoked pot and cried. Ike and Howard were African-Americans from the Chicago area; they were stunned and overwhelmed, as was I. The shooting of JFK, and now MLK, were two events that changed history. The Civil Rights Movement was to gain power, and all races needed to examine their place in the movement.

I ended up flunking out of Carthage and going into the Air Force. One good thing that I got out of Carthage was my ex-wife, Judy. We dated and fell in love and had two wonderful children, Heidi and Ginni. We both were young and somewhat naive about life; how Judy put up with my behaviors over the years is beyond me!

My GPA for Carthage was a whopping .06 average. What a wreck I was at Carthage! I now was going to get married and head for basic training, which was a long way from going into the ministry!

Judy and I were married on October 12, 1968. On December 10, 1968 I went into the USAF. I went to basic training at Lackland Air Force Base in Texas; basic was an eye opener for me. Going into the service helped my organizational skills, self-concept, and discipline in general; however, the ADHD problems of anxiety, focusing, and task completing were my partners all the way through basic training. My obsessive-compulsive disorder and depression were still present, and they were issues that I needed to deal with in order to become healthy. To this day, I am amazed that I functioned on any level with all the negative issues that I was not addressing. Even more amazing was the fact that no one ever told me that I had a drinking problem or emotional issues. I only knew that I had severe problems; but I did not discern how to address them correctly by seeing a psychologist, counselor, or even a medical doctor. Again I want to stress how important it is to get an early diagnosis of the disorder of ADHD, so treatment can start immediately. Carrying ADHD from a youth into adulthood is the harbinger of a difficult life.

In the service, I was assigned as squad leader. However, my spinning and swirling mind took me out of that position quickly. I could not concentrate on the directions that I needed to give the troops. My TI (or training instructor) demoted me in a nice way. He said, "Ron, you have too much on your mind." I have to laugh now. Yes, I had a mind that was overloaded and stimulated in ways that neither Sgt. Carter nor I realized. What I liked about Sgt. Carter was that he saw some positive traits in me and accepted me for who I was at the time -- hurting, but a nice man.

During basic, we had to march in competition with other squadrons. I was such a terrible marcher that Sgt. Carter asked me to be road guard. The road guards did not participate in the marching ceremony. While our squadron was marching, we had to wait for them outside of the parade grounds. Guess what? I lost my squadron! My attention was not on the parade, I was dreaming of other things in life; my ADHD tendencies were alive and well. My mind was flipping and flopping like pancakes being turned on a hot grill. My gross motor skills were just not jiving with my mind; my coordination was not good when I was young, and that was a part of my physical state as I advanced into adulthood.

Initially, when I entered basic I was a hefty 230 pounds. Tech Sgt. Carter put me up in front of the squadron and made me exercise all that excessive fat off. I worked very hard to lose all the weight; there were only two of us in the squadron that were asked to go up into the remedial group of "fatties." I lost thirty pounds, so exercising up in front of the group helped me out.

During basic we were required to memorize the Military Code of Conduct. My short term memory and memorization skills in general were still not doing well. I was relieved that none of the sergeants in basic asked me many questions! The fear of failing had been with me since elementary school. Failures earlier in my life were affecting me profoundly in adulthood. Basic training passed, and I came out a better person. I lost thirty pounds, felt great about the person I was becoming, and I could run a mile in under eight minutes.

After basic, I went to Kessler AFB in Mississippi for more training. While at Kessler, I continued my drinking and poor behavior. Judy and I were young and needed stability, yet I was unable to give that stability to Judy or myself. I was not acting like an adult, I would say "yes" in making promises, and then change my mind; I was getting out of shape after I got in shape in basic and not giving Judy what she deserved: love and respect. How could I love someone else, when I did not love myself?

From Kessler, I went on to Tinker AFB, Oklahoma, Vietnam, and then to Colorado for my duty stations. While in the service, I had two beautiful daughters, Heidi and Ginni. The medical bills for both girls' births totaled fourteen dollars! The service had good medical benefits.

Heidi was born February 1, 1970. She had beautiful brown hair and blue eyes. The beautiful baby was born on Tinker AFB, Oklahoma, so she was officially an Okie. Her smile was very radiant, and it still is today!

Ginni, my younger daughter, was born on April 27, 1972 in Aurora Colorado at Fitzsimmons Military Hospital. The day Ginni was born there was a major blizzard in Colorado. We were lucky that our living quarters were just across the street from where she was born. I recall simply walking over to the hospital, as it was too dangerous to drive in the snow.

Another related ADHD situation happened when Ginni was born. I was in the waiting room at the hospital while my wife was in labor and soon to give birth to my second daughter. After several hours, the nurses brought a brown headed baby who looked so cute right past me into the recovery room. I was soon told it was my daughter who was taken past me into a space with other newborns. I thought that the nurse had told me to go ahead and go into the room to see the baby. Well, I went into the room and started walking around. Back in the 1970s we could not be with the mother and baby during birth, and we certainly could not be in the recovery room! Soon nurses came in and asked me if I was a doctor; they stated that only doctors could be in the restricted area. Here is one time that my poor listening skills were to my benefit! I was gently escorted back outside into the hallway. I could observe Ginni through the windows of the nursery.

After my duty in Colorado, I got an early discharge to go back to college. I wanted to take advantage of the GI Bill and do something that I enjoyed doing; however, I did not know at the time that I would go into the teaching profession. I wanted to go into some kind of social work where I could help people and make a difference in others' lives.

On September 12, 1972, we loaded the truck and headed for Illinois State University in Normal, Illinois. I was scared to death going to a large university. I knew I had to take care of my family and make sure they were healthy -- I could not afford to fail. Without a job or income, I would be putting my family in big trouble.

The first two years at ISU, I did very well. However, I learned to play the game of selecting the teachers who fit my learning style the best. I talked to students on campus about the professors and their teaching styles and expectations. My strengths were in writing, public speaking, and note-taking. I tried to stay away from those professors who just gave multiple choice tests. I especially enjoyed the profs who gave tests from their notes and not so much from reading the textbooks. Reflecting back to junior college, I used the study skills that Mr. Peace, my psychology teacher, introduced to me; they helped me out tremendously.

My disorder of hyper-focusing helped me during lectures. I took notes quickly while tuning all distractions out of my mind. I actually had other students asking me for my notes to copy. My note-taking skills and writing skills were two key attributes that helped me get through college.

I was lucky to have a smart wife in Judy. She knew the English language very well. Back in the 1970s, we did not have spell check and grammar check, among the many other technological advantages relating to the computer. Like a smart person for once, I delegated Judy to read and correct my papers. I got As on most of my term papers. One thing we can do today as ADHDers is to hire people to make up for our weaknesses that we have in certain areas. We need to discover what our strengths are, and use them to our advantage. I would have been in big trouble if Judy had refused to correct my papers. Thank you, Judy, for your patience and great English skills!

While at ISU, I used a manual typewriter to type my reports! Can you imagine a hyperactive individual typing with an old manual typewriter? I used to make errors upon errors in typing; I would have to take the eraser and try not to smudge the paper. This was hopeless for me. So again, I hired other students to type my work! I used to have piles upon piles of papers by my side, all torn out from the typewriter in frustration when I made mistakes in my typing! It is critical, as an ADHDer, to know your strengths and weaknesses. Today, there are several kinds of inventories which you can take to allow you to see what you are talented and not so gifted at.

I ended my first year with a 3.0 average and did very well. I was proud that I turned my life around and proved to myself I was not stupid. I was on the Dean's list every semester. During the first year I decided to major in Sociology-Anthropology and to minor in Social Work and Psychology. I enjoyed studying these areas and did well in them.

While at ISU, I was still dealing with my ADHD symptoms and drinking a lot. This was damaging my marriage. I was self-centered, and did not take responsibility for being a good dad and encouraging my children as I should. Drinking in front of them was not positive role modeling for a father to do. I did, however, read to the girls, took them places, and was a good dad in many areas of parenting. I knew I did not want my daughters to grow up and have the emotional issues that I dealt with all my life. I enjoyed taking the girls on picnics and to the parks down in Bloomington, Illinois.

My lack of self-esteem, poor exercise habits, and low tolerance for frustration were taking a heavy toll on my marriage. It takes a very strong lady to put up with someone who has ADHD; Judy went way beyond what she had to do. She had two children as it was -- adding me as a third child to raise was not good.

My second year at ISU went well, and I continued to make the Dean's List. I enjoyed it when the news was sent back to the local newspaper in Freeport that I had been a success. I wanted every one of those teachers and coaches who thought I was lazy to read the damn article!

During the1973-1974 school year, Judy went back to school; we both shared in the responsibility of taking care of Heidi and Ginni. It was fun for me to watch and play with the girls. We lived in married student housing at Cardinal Court in Normal. The girls would help me plant a community garden in the spring time, behind the apartments. This was a special time for dad and the daughters to do some bonding.

I continued to do well in school despite my drinking to help medicate my ADHD; only God knows how I got through those years. I ended up getting my BS degree in 1974 in Sociology-Anthropology, and I had two minors: one in psychology and the other in social work.

Judy had one year of college left, so I decided to go for my master's degree. I was accepted into the College of Education, and Judy finished her degree in home economics. I completed my MS Degree in Education in 1976. I had to take my comprehensive examinations; here is where my writing skills would be judged critically by the professors. I knew the material very well and had all the necessary information down to pass the exam. At the time of the examination, I did not realize that the professors would be grading on grammar, sentence structure, and vocabulary along with the content.

After taking the exam, I was quite confident that I had passed, and knew all the information that was presented before me. To my surprise, I was called in by all of the professors; they were going to fail me because of my poor grammar and spelling. As I mentioned earlier, my ex-wife Judy, did all the grammar checking for me on my papers while in undergraduate and graduate school. However, she could not do that for me when I was taking the comprehensive exams. The professors scolded me for my poor grammar and lack of sentence structure. I want to point out that the errors were not that numerous, but I failed to meet the expectations of the graduate department and committee.

I had taken graduate courses from all the professors on the committee and received As. One of the professors yelled at me and said that a third grader would know how to write better than I did on the exam. She was exactly right; my ADHD characteristics prevented me from learning what I needed to know as a youngster. I missed out on a large amount of what was being taught to me because of my inattention and lack of focus in elementary school and beyond.

During 1976, I was getting my family ready to move; we needed to have all things in order to move on for my first job. We did not have much money to make our move; I could not screw up and be retained for another semester by failing the exam. We would certainly be in financial hardship.

Reflecting back on my experience at ISU, I become angry about the way I was treated. How could the professors give me As and yet grade me on a few grammatical errors? I gave speeches in their classes and completed projects, yet they did not recognize any of my "weaknesses." How could a university have such tunnel vision about their policies?

As of 1976, I did not know that I had ADHD but I realized that something was wrong, as I was still experiencing depression and anxiety. I wanted help with my problems, but I was so "out of focus" about where I was in my life and the direction I was headed. The points I like to stress are my earlier educational and ADHD problems would not go away until I addressed them head on. However, I first needed to know something was wrong, and not be in a state of denial as I had been all of my life.

The committees asked me to rewrite the exam and do the best I could with the grammar. I rewrote the examination and I did not do better. How could I? I did not know the simple third-grade rules of grammar and sentence structure!

Dr. Smith, the committee chairlady, called me in and told me I had to assure her that I would never go on for a Ph.D. I told her that I would not go on for the doctorate. In my heart, I felt I would go on if I wanted to, but I would say whatever she wanted to hear. I had a family and needed to move on with my life.

It is quite amazing that I graduated from graduate school with all my drinking and depression. I know the depression and drinking had to have influenced the way I thought and studied. The vexations or residuals of ADHD continued to be on my back in 1976.

In the spring of 1977, my family and I were off to Oak Creek, Wisconsin. I accepted a position as a special education teacher instructing behavior disordered children. This was to be a mess. How can a screwed up ADHDer be teaching children who had severe emotional and behavioral issues? When I went to Oak Creek High School to teach, the behavior disorder program was just starting out. I had days when no one would show up to class. I was helping to start the program, and I felt uncomfortable at Oak Creek doing what I was hired to do -- that is, mainly plan a program and teach three or four students a day.

I decided to put an application in at the Board of Education in Rockford, Illinois for a BD (behavioral disorder) teacher. I went for the interview and was accepted into the district as a teacher.

I started the 1978-1979 school year at Wilson Middle School. I had a class of five students. They were a challenging group to handle. I started a behavior modification program and the first year went well. Many of my students had severe emotional and social problems. Not much academic teaching was going on; it was mainly behavior management and helping the students to realize they had potential. I ended up teaching at Wilson Middle School for only two years. In 1980, I transferred to Swan Hillman Elementary School, where I taught fourth grade in a regular education class.

The school year I started at Hillman was 1980-1981. I was hired to teach fourth graders. In my first class, I had 23 fourth graders; they were a lovely group. After teaching at-risk children for two years, I felt it was a piece of cake instructing regular education students!

Dealing with my ADHD issues was very challenging as I grew older. I was in my early thirties and still did not know what was wrong with my mind. I was not mature, and my mind still raced, yet at a higher speed. I complained and was never happy; my mind still chronically wandered, I was unfocused, into myself, and did not give to my marriage as I should have. I needed to be emotionally present for my wife and children, and I was not. I was trying to figure out why I was afraid to allow others to know the real me. Ironically, I did not yet know who I really was as a teacher, father, and man.

The first two school years at Hillman were great as a teacher. I had a good administrator, good teacher friends, and great students. The families were very supportive and loving. They wanted their children to have the best education and I wanted to be part of that process. I enjoyed teaching my students through the VAKT methodology. I learned this method from studying in graduate school. When writing my lesson plans and objectives, I would be sure to include activities that included the visual, auditory, kinesthetic, and tactical learning modalities. Grace Fernald was the person who introduced this method in helping special needs students. I plainly thought this method would be effective in teaching children with all ability levels. I did not want anyone to be excluded from learning, like I had been when I was younger.

During my second year of teaching at Hillman, I met a special teacher and human. Her name was Barb Johnson. Barb taught second grade at Swan Hillman and was an excellent teacher. At the start of each year, I wanted to get to know my students; I did this by having them write an essay about their lives. Several of the students mentioned Mrs. Johnson, their second grade teacher. They told me how she had been fighting breast cancer and how much they enjoyed having her as a teacher. I was so moved that we sent Mrs. Johnson cards wishing her well; the students told her how much they cared for her as a teacher.

The letter-writing by the students was to be the start of a long and enduring friendship between Barb and me. We talked endless hours on the phone, went on shopping trips together, and became very close friends. The friendship we had was a soul mate type of acquaintance. For some reason, Barb was the first friend who really understood where I was coming from; she saw the real deal in my personality that others did not observe.

During 1983, a major event happened in my life; Barb was there for me as a friend and ended up being my mentor and coach. My marriage to Judy was ending. She was worn out from my poor behavior as a husband. For fifteen years Judy put up with my chronic wandering mind, broken promises, my self-medicating with alcohol, being into myself and not listening to her concerns. Judy told me she wanted a divorce. At this point in my life, I was a worn down ADHDer who did not know what was wrong. Year after year of playing and listening to the same old songs in my mind wore and tore me down physically, mentally, and spiritually. God brought me to my knees; I ended up in the hospital for two weeks.

During the two weeks in the hospital, I did a self-assessment. I knew that I would have to change my life or I would not be around long. During the next two years, I found out that I could become strong and become a better human. Barb Johnson, and my two daughters Heidi and Ginni, gave me strength to grow and become more self-actualized. About four years after I was hospitalized, Barb died of cancer. She had been a special person, helping me with my recovery process.

Just before Barb died, I was going to move into a new apartment. One of the teachers I worked with told me that he would help me move; however, he broke his promise. He was supposed to get his dad's truck and help out. I was grateful for his offer. I did not have much money and needed to find friends to assist me. However, this friend did not follow through. It was a cold January day when I was to move; he called me at the last moment and said he could not lend a hand in the severe cold. I was literally "out in the cold." I had to be out of my apartment and into my new one on this Saturday. I called Barb and told her my dilemma and she responded. She told me that she would get her dad's truck to help me move. This was to be two weeks before Barb died.

Barb and her dad showed up on that cold January day and helped me out. She could barely climb the steps to get to the second floor. She looked like a skeleton, had dark rings around her eyes, and bent over while climbing the steps. If I had to give a definition of friendship, I would say "Barb Johnson." She was caring, compassionate, unselfish -- and, while dying, helped a friend out. As I mentioned, it was two weeks after I moved into the Rockton Avenue apartment when Barb died. She was my angel in life and showed me how to live and celebrate life until death. The ironic thing about Barb dying at Rockford Memorial Hospital was that I lived right next door.

How could it be that I moved and then Barb would die right next door to the place where she helped me move? God works in strange and wonderful ways. I went to Barb's funeral, and when Barb was buried, so was a large part of me. I promised myself by living the longest life that I could, by being a good teacher, learning to love all people, and giving my heart to God, Barb would live through me.

I spent more than ten years teaching at Swan Hillman. It was great that I was in a profession that allowed me to move around and be creative. My ADHD positive attributes such as "out of the box thinking," being a maverick, and also a crazy, funny person helped me to be an excellent teacher. So there are some great things about having ADHD!

During my stint at Hillman, I was prescribed Prozac to help with my chemical problems. I also ended up finding a great psychologist and psychiatrist. The psychologist, Dr. Mcardle, and the psychiatrist, Dr. William Wood, both had an integral part in helping me to become healthy.

At Swan Hillman, I was the number one requested teacher according to my administrators. This was very humbling, and made me feel like I had something to offer, despite the person that I was! The parents and students were kind and accepting to me as a teacher. As an educator, I enjoyed making creative bulletin boards and implementing a variety of teaching strategies. Teaching was not a job; it was a fun way to live!

In 1991 I left Swan Hillman and went to Westview Elementary School. I enjoyed my two years at Westview. Randy Larson was the principal; he was an excellent leader and communicator with his teachers. He was pro teacher all the way and loved to get the students involved with the community. Annually, Randy would have parades to a local nursing home. In addition, he recruited mentors from the nursing home to work with the students. Randy brought to life what education should be all about: working and studying with the community at large -- in this case, the senior citizens.

While at Swan Hillman, I was nominated twice to *Who's Who Among American Teachers.* In order to nominate a teacher, the students had to be in the top five percent of their high school graduating class! This was very humbling for me as a teacher and ADHD person, that someone recognized me! I thought, "I have come a long way from the elementary days when the teachers and administrators thought I was retarded."

While at Westview, I was nominated again to *Who's Who Among American Teachers.*This would be the third time out of six that I would be elected by former students! By the way, all of the former students were from my elementary school teaching years, and none from middle school. I found this to be very surprising, that the youngsters would remember me from way back in elementary school.

I was now smiling and feeling wonderful about the person I was becoming. Hey, a kid that was supposed to be retarded, a slow learner, and one who graduated at the lower end of his class was now finding who he really was as a human; he was being recognized by others.

Something wonderful and magical occurred while I was at Westview School. The local newspaper, the *Rockford Register Star*, came and interviewed me about my nomination to *Who's Who Among American Teachers*. They took photos and interviewed me about the students and the award I was given. The article was later published in the paper. My former sixth grade teacher, Mrs. Eckhart, read the article and came to say hello and thank you to me. I mentioned Mrs. Eckhart previously in the book and how she touched my life decades earlier. She was honored that I mentioned her as a teacher who made a great difference in my life. I took Mrs. E. out for lunch, and we had a wonderful talk. She invited me to her horse ranch, but I never got in touch with her to do so.

I taught at Westview for two short years when an opportunity came along for me to apply for a job in the sixth grade at a school, Marsh Elementary, that was just opening. I found this to be a chance to get in on the ground floor and help establish a school improvement plan. While at Marsh, I was teaching with some top notch teachers and an excellent principal, Cheryl Foltz. She gave me the freedom to teach the way I wanted. I had the opportunity to teach poetry and language arts to all of the sixth graders; poetry is my passion.

My love for poetry began when I started to go to my psychologist, Renee Mcardle. She encouraged me to journal and write verses to express myself; I fell in love with poetry and read widely. Some of my favorite poets are Carl Sandburg, e.e. cummings, Langston Hughes, and Robert Frost. Penning poetry was a gift that I never knew I possessed; writing was good therapy for dealing with my ADHD symptoms and traits.

Robert Frost made a comment, "A good poem begins in delight and ends in wisdom." I etched that statement into my mind to stay forever and to base much of my prose upon. To me, Frost was stating that a poem that was delightful would immediately catch the reader's attention. The reader would become deep in thought and get wisdom from reading the poem in its entirety. I told my students they could take the poet's wisdom and apply it to their lives. I taught my students that wisdom is different than learning; in wisdom you take what you have learned and apply it to your life so it can be meaningful.

I immersed the students in poetry and literature; I established a poetry cafe and invited the parents and students from the different grade levels in to watch. We included the entire school in viewing our production. Students used their artistic abilities and made the background for the poets while they recited their poetry. Most students had dual roles; they were artists and recited poems. The theme of the presentations centered on Robert Frost and Langston Hughes: both poets whom we studied in detail. We included the parents in helping us organize and build the cafe atmosphere. One dad made a stage for the students to stand on, and another purchased candles (battery operated) to place on the tables. We placed red and white plastic checkered tablecloths on all the tables; we put four desks together to make a square for tables. Next, we typed up programs and a student handed them out to the audience as they filed into the classroom. In addition, we had a parent tape record our performances. It was a big success and the children learned much about art, literature, math, and English from the project. This is an example of how I used the VAKT method of teaching in elementary school, and also the multiple intelligences theory.

Years later, I got a letter from one of my students who was attending college. Adam S. wrote to me from the University of Florida; he shared with me how poetry had touched his life. He told me how poetry was a doorway to liking literature in college. He said he especially enjoyed writing poetry to his lady friends. Adam is now a successful dentist. I wonder if he has poems that he's written displayed on the walls for his patients to view.

The first group of students I taught at Marsh were very talented and gifted in the arts. I enjoyed the students' zest to be active in learning and have fun at what they were doing. For the spring program, we presented poetry to the parents from all the sixth graders.

I had a chance to recite some of my poetry, and the students did a wonderful job with choral poetry!

As one of Frost's poems states, "I took the road less traveled by and that has made all the difference." This quote applies to my way of thinking as an ADDer and my teaching style, as well as my life.

I taught at Marsh for three years. I learned and grew from exceptional peers that I taught with, as well as from my students and their parents. The parental involvement was key to my success as a teacher. While at Marsh, I met my second wife. I had been divorced from Judy for eleven years. My second marriage lasted only four years, as some tragic events in our lives led to an unstable marriage. My first divorce was my fault, as I was struggling with my disorder of ADHD. However, the second time, outside circumstances beyond my control contributed to the fall of the marriage.

After the divorce from my second wife, I wanted to examine myself as a human and grow as much as I could. I continued my counseling and tried to understand myself more. This is when I found out that I had ADHD. I went into Dr. Mcardle, whom I was now calling Renee, and told her that I read a book on attention deficit disorder and noticed I displayed some of the characteristics that defined ADHD. The frequency, duration, and intensity of behaviors I displayed were much more than my peers. I was highly distractible, very impulsive, and restless in my body and mind.

Renee, my psychologist, scheduled an appointment for me to be tested. The battery of tests at that time was a family history, intelligence test, and how my behaviors were throughout my life. Some of the questions the psychologist asked me came from the DSM of psychology which is used in helping to derive a diagnosis; I believe other questions came from the ADHD Rating Scale. I did not include my primary doctor in any of the rating; I felt that my psychologist and psychiatrist possessed enough expertise about ADHD. However, I did get a blood panel and a complete physical; these tests came out fine.

The other problems that I was experiencing, along with my ADHD symptoms, were examined. They were: my comprehension problems, substance abuse, post-traumatic stress disorder, anxiety, and depression. A week later, after taking the tests, I was called to get the results. The psychologist told me that I had ADHD! This was a big relief in my mind, body, and soul. The questions that I had for years about the way I acted were answered. I went out the door happy and said, "Yes, I have ADHD!"

Knowing I was diagnosed with ADHD, I could now do something about the residuals and comorbid conditions that I was fighting. At the age of fifty, I finally found out what was wrong with me -- however, waiting fifty years to do something about my disorder was way too long to wait!

As a teacher, if there were indications that a student had ADHD, I would refer the student to a psychologist and a multidisciplinary team. Many times parents ignored my concerns and therefore ignored their children's mental, physical, and spiritual health. I would keep a written record of observable behaviors and frequency of behaviors to present to the multidisciplinary team. Our team usually was made up of the teachers, psychologist, social worker, nurse, and one administrator. It is critical that a child gets help if he or shows signs of ADHD or the conditions that go along with the traits or disorder. The longer that ADHD goes undiagnosed, the worse it will get for the student as they advance or do not advance in their academic career. With me, the conditions just got worse as I went from childhood into adulthood because they were not addressed.

I taught many ADHD students; for the most part, they were very bright and gifted. Numerous students were lost in the cracks of the educational system because the schools were not addressing their unique learning styles. Today, many teachers instruct through the multiple intelligences, which addresses the diverse population of students they instruct. As a teacher, it was critical that I assess each student's learning style and how they processed information.

Many of the ADHD students I taught were gifted in the arts. Sad to say, the arts were cut back and many never got to realize their gifts. I question why school districts cut the arts, as they are critical in the total development of a person. Budget cuts are not an excuse; we will pay dearly for not educating a student down the road -- either by the student dropping out of school or getting in trouble with the law; a balanced educational system is needed.

In the last five years, I have read in the newspaper about two of my former ADHD students dying. They were very gifted; however, their disorders where not properly addressed. One died from an overdose of drugs; he was twenty-one. The other shot himself in the head; he was lost and empty in his life. To me, this is a tragedy, and we all must take a hard look at the facts. Another one of my students dropped out of school; he was a very gifted artist. Families, teachers, and society must come together and act on this epidemic, ADHD, that we have today. The numbers vary, but it is estimated that between eight and fifteen million adults in the United States alone are walking around with undiagnosed ADHD.

I stayed at Marsh for three years; I had the itch for change so I applied for a position at Walker Elementary School. As an ADDer, I did not mind change; in fact, I was elated that I was in a career that allowed me to transform what I was doing and have diversity. ADDers get bored quickly; I craved variety and stimulation when I taught students.

I found out I had ADHD after my second marriage. It was a blessing; now I could focus on change and move forward in my life. I had to be proactive in altering many of the residual problems that came along with my ADHD, as well as reducing the hallmark symptoms of impulsivity, distractibility, and restlessness. ADDers are good at selecting the wrong mates; I doubted that I would ever take the leap of marriage again.

After my divorce I enrolled in night classes at Northern Illinois University in DeKalb, Illinois. Not only did the classes increase my knowledge in education, but helped me on the pay scale. In addition, I got involved in workshops on literature and poetry. One seminar I attended was hosted by the school district in which I was working, District #205 in Rockford, Illinois. We broke down into discussion groups and each group was to write a poem. We wrote a group poem; the group asked me to share one of the poems that I wrote in my diary. I created a poem, *Keep in Touch with Your Dreams*. The poem's main theme was to never give up on your dreams. It took me fifty years to actualize some of my dreams I thought would never come true. Here is the poem that I presented to my fellow teachers:

Keep in touch with your dreams,
For they are yours alone.
They are glittering stars within your mind and soul.
Put wings on your dreams and soar to new heights,
For in life's clouds your dreams will appear.
Cup your hands and do not fear,
Those magical dreams will brightly appear,
Only if you believe in your dreams!

After reciting the poem, one of the participants came over and asked me to write the poem down for her. I told her that I would be honored to write it down. I scribbled the verses on a piece of paper; as I handed her my poem, tears welled up in her eyes. She shared with me that a good friend of hers was in the hospital dying of breast cancer; she wanted to take the poem and share it with her friend. I was humbled and elated at the same time; I knew that one of my poems was going to comfort the heart of one who was suffering from a terrible disease that I hate.

I started teaching at Walker in 1995 and remained there for two years before transferring to Eisenhower Middle School. I enjoyed teaching in the elementary schools, but I thought middle school students would be fun and challenging. I was correct -- the students and parents were fantastic! At Eisenhower, I had a great administrator in Yolanda Simmons. She was fair and expected a lot; after teaching at Eisenhower for eight years, I retired from teaching in 2005.

Throughout my years at Eisenhower, I taught U.S. History to eighth graders. I instructed through the multiple intelligence approach, as created by Howard Gardner. He defined seven basic intelligences that people possessed; today, there are several more intelligences that are recognized. The seven intelligences are: logical-mathematical, musical-rhythmic, verbal-linguistic, visual-spatial, bodily-kinesthetic, intra-personal, and inter-personal intelligence. An eighth and ninth -- naturalistic, and existential -- have been added to Gardner's original seven intelligences.

When I was in elementary school, it would have helped if I had been taught with the various intelligences in mind. My ADHD positive characteristics could have been recognized and therefore,

I would have grown as a student. The only intelligence test, the Stanford-Binet, was used as a measure of what we knew. Today, many teachers are aware of the benefits of providing a curriculum that embraces the multiple intelligences and the VAKT method of Grace Fernald. By teaching through diverse methods, you are tapping into the students' strengths and weaknesses, therefore, challenging all ability levels.

I integrated the arts, physical education, public speaking, debate, science, and theatre into teaching history. By teaching across the curriculum, I reinforced many of the concepts that were taught in other core classes. It was nice to see the students responding in positive ways. I not only gave tests, but provided an array of measurement techniques to evaluate the students; including having each child create a portfolio of their work.

At the beginning of the year, I provided the students with the multiple intelligences survey. I evaluated the outcome of the surveys, and the students and I would go over the results; the learner became aware of their strengths and areas they did not prefer. As a special needs person, I understood both the slow learner and the gifted child; I am convinced that ADHD made me a better teacher, and more empathetic with the students and parents.

During the 1999-2000 school year, I was nominated by students for the Golden Apple. This is when students or other teachers nominate a teacher for their excellence in teaching; I was flattered, and accepted the process which all the teachers that are recommended had to go through. We were required to put pen to paper and write essays and get recommendations from teachers and parents. I was elated that I was in the final fifteen nominated. I did not receive the Golden Apple, but since I was in the final fifteen, we automatically became part of the academy. Today, there about four hundred teachers in the academy; my wife, Lisa, is also a part of the honored group.

My methods of teaching with the multiple intelligences and VAKT techniques thrilled the students and parents. Numerous students have written to me over the years sharing with me how much they enjoyed the way I taught U.S. History. I am not sharing these comments with you in a boastful manner; I want to point out that how you teach is as important as what you teach when dealing with a diverse population!

At Eisenhower, when school was out in the spring, students had the opportunity to write letters of thanks to any teacher who had influenced their lives. The note is titled, *You Make a Difference*. Over the years I have received well over three hundred letters. I have included some of the letters in this book. I have omitted the names of the students to respect their privacy. The students had a way in helping me through my ADHD by writing sincere letters. The pain of suffering all my life is lightened by the love the students have shown to me.

Knowing how I suffered from the ADHD that I endured over the years, I did not want any of the students in my class to have any negative educational experiences. I asked all my students to respect each other with dignity, be compassionate for one another, and reach out and assist each other when needed. My attitude was to teach my students as Jesus Christ would teach them. I shared with my students that each of us has good and bad characteristics, that no one was better than anyone else; we all have our Achilles' heel!

I never was too big to apologize to the class if I acted in an inappropriate way as a teacher; I offered open and two way communication with my students. I took time to talk with the students in the hallways before and after school and in the lunchroom. This paid major dividends; the students grew to trust me as a person who was genuine and cared for them as unique people.

I know that words are powerful landmines; they can explode and destroy a person's self-concept; we all want to be admired and loved. Taking time with my students showed that I cared, and promoted a special student-teacher relationship. Acts of kindness and not feigning love are keys to lasting relationships in all areas of our lives.

Over my many years of teaching, I eavesdropped on teachers bragging about how difficult their exams were, that many students failed them. I asked myself, "What are these people doing in the teaching profession?" If a number of students are failing a teacher's exams, the professor is failing too! The material should be taught in such a meaningful way that all students grasp the information.

I enjoyed my years at Eisenhower. During my time teaching at the middle school, my mother was diagnosed with breast cancer; I was her primary caretaker. My sister helped out as much as she could; Sherry lives in California, so it was difficult for her to be here on a steady basis. Like most of us, as our parents get older, we become the parents and they become the child. When the parent gets ill, it is challenging, yet worth every minute to be by their side and offer love and support. The old disorder, fear, popped into my brain and anxiety started to become visible; the "what if" vexations ruminated in my mind, causing increasing anxiety and panic.

After Mom died in 2001, I began having panic attacks along with my PTSD coming alive; I again needed to rest my weary mind. I took time off from school and received additional therapy and regained balance in my life. Looking back, I had courage to do the right thing, although it was painful. I always wondered what others thought about me. In the end, God guided my way to a healthier and happy life. It is not so important what others think when you know what is best for your life. Others did not know who I really was inside.

In 2005 I decided to retire; I was ready to go on to another kind of life. The district was offering first-rate incentives to retire. Teaching had been good to me; however, I wanted to switch gears and try embracing a different lifestyle. I was extremely happy going into retirement. I gave 110 percent for most of my career. Teaching is a great profession, but a very demanding one. An educator plays many roles: instructor of curriculum, nurse, psychologist, social worker, father, mother. It was time that I give more attention to myself and family.

In May of 2005 we had a big retirement party given by the school district. The event was a lot of fun; I had the opportunity to see educators whom I had not been in contact with for several years.

The first years of retirement were an adjustment for me. I worked out more, read and did more writing. I got involved with others and helped out at the local YMCA. I wanted to give back what God had given me. I participated in the Chicago Marathon for two years in a row. I raised money with the help of generous friends for the American Cancer Society and Children's Memorial Hospital in Chicago.

Truthfully, I thought I would never get married again; but in

2006 God put Lisa into my life. Her sister's father-in-law, Jeff Cote, was working at the YMCA. We talked about each other's lives and became friends. Jeff is an easy and loving man to talk to and share stories with as a friend; he told me he knew someone that he thought I might enjoy meeting. Jeff arranged a date for Lisa and me during June of 2006. Lisa and I met for dinner and the rest is history. We dated for a year and then decided to get married; Lisa and I became instant soul mates. That is, we both have a deep love for Christ and life. Moreover, she understands this ADHD person, which takes a lot of energy and compassion. We both agree that marriage is about working as a team toward common and individual goals. Lisa helps me refocus and continue to work on my issues of ADHD. She has been an excellent wife, teacher, coach, and mentor.

As an ADHD person, I realize that life is not all about me! I tend to hyper-focus on myself at times, which is not good. I realize that my actions and attitudes affect my relationship with Lisa. I try to work one day at a time, growing as an individual and as a couple. The greatest attribute of my wife is that she is an excellent listener; I do not need Lisa to solve my ADHD issues -- I need to do that! What she offers me is a loving heart and listening ears, and a heart that listens with empathy and compassion.

It is now 2010, and Lisa and I have been married for three years. Life has been going well for both of us. Lisa teaches music at one of the local elementary schools, and loves what she does. She reminds me daily of what teaching entails, which is a love for her students and wanting to be the best she can be as a teacher and role model. Like many educators, Lisa goes beyond what is required of her. She keeps up on her expertise as a music teacher by taking college courses; she takes students on field trips, communicates with parents, and works to help each student master the goals established by the school district and state. In addition, Lisa plays in a wind ensemble, bands birds, and is a grandmother. She has a passion and love for music and nature. I cannot keep up with her! For over twenty years, Lisa had banded and identified birds at a local bird sanctuary. She knows Latin names of the birds and can tell you immediately what kind of bird is making a call. Lisa is an active environmentalist and supports the issues of global warming.

I have been retired going on five years. Presently I have goals to help others by speaking about ADHD and telling my life story. There are so many people in our society who do not know they have ADHD as a disorder, or traits that have to be confronted. It is my goal to make a difference and let the community know it is ok to be different and how important it is to know their strengths as well as weaknesses to be successful and feel healthy.

Next, I would like to list the behaviors that I have fought for sixty-two years and make a brief comment about those ADHD traits and disorders.

Like many people of my generation, I have journeyed a long and difficult path with undiagnosed ADHD. Some of my ADHD traits have been more severe than others, therefore becoming disorders. If the trait intensely influences and affects your life, then you have a major disorder that must be confronted and dealt with by professionals. Some negative traits I have handled by immersing myself in literature and making the necessary changes; I've had to talk to a psychologist and psychiatrist to help me out. Traits can become disorders if you do not deal with the issues. Below are positive and negative traits I have experienced.

1. *Perseveration* -- Worry and fear created my perseveration. Anxiety to me became toxic; I would dwell on problems, real or imagined. It was very difficult to stop the spinning records. The end result was that I was withdrawing from the world and trapped in my own world of distortions.My relationships suffered, and I was not growing as an individual. By embracing positive affirmations, hanging around positive people, and having a strong faith in God, I have eliminated this vexation. In addition, counseling and medication have helped me to focus. Getting out with others and getting more involved in social situations has helped promote a healthy mind.

2. *Anxiety* -- I did not know how to enjoy and relax in life. I had to have everything "now." I always rushed into decision making, hurried to appointments, hastily eating and drinking to help calm my worries and anxieties, and lived in a constant

state of fear. The wiggly worms that crawled through my mind and body were always there to make me squirm. It was a constant peak-and-valley experience. Drinking and eating obsessively only made things worse. I got better by stopping drinking, exercising, having more faith in God, and changing my diet. I started networking with people more to celebrate life by teaching as well as learning from others. In addition, I started reading positive literature and staying away from television and its vicissitudes.

3. *Obsessive Compulsive Disorder* -- Because of almost dying and having a fear of death as well as life, I developed OCD at a very early age. I believe that the neurology of my mind changed in a way to affect the way I thought. For example, at a young age I did not want to throw away paper because of my fingerprints on the paper. I felt that I was losing a part of who I was. Again, focusing on the good and not the bad has helped me with the disorder. I really had to work hard with OCD.

4. *Temper outbursts* -- At a young age and later in my adult life, I would become frustrated because I did not know what to do about the internal turmoil I was experiencing. If things did not go my way, I would become moody and angry. When I was young, the neighborhood kids would tease me about my big head and I would want to fight them. Aggression was a part of my behavior that was damaging me physically and mentally. Today I have outgrown my temper outbursts. Psychotherapy and talking out my past helped me deal with this issue.

5. *Cheating* -- I cheated on exams in junior high and high school because I was tired of failure and wanted to be recognized. This is not an excuse for what I did, but a reason. I knew that I was smart. If I was not aware of how I could correct my way of thinking, what else could I do? I was learning how to exist at a very expensive cost: my mental, spiritual, and physical health.

By experiencing small successes in my life and meeting people who genuinely cared about me, I gained confidence in my abilities. I got to know how I learned best and how my mind responded to different ways of learning.

6. *Short term memory* -- It was very painful for me to learn; with all the emotional baggage I carried, I found it difficult to learn anything. By breaking learning down into smaller segments, both my short-term and long-term memory improved greatly. By dealing with my issues of impulsivity, restlessness, and distractibility, my mind has become clearer and I am focusing better.

7. *High mental and physical energy* -- As a youngster and as an adult, I have always had energy to burn. My dad used to constantly tell me that I had "ants in my pants." I have harnessed my energy through exercise, diet, and developing a positive attitude about life.

8. *Generosity to a fault* -- I am smiling as I am writing this; I have a heart as big as the state of Texas. I give way too much to others to this day. I probably will never become "less" generous. As an ADDer, I yearn to be a part of others by loving and understanding them. I have learned, however, to think about how much and to whom I give money!

9. *Proving myself to others* -- Because of my constant failures and being teased as a youngster, I always felt I was not good enough for others. I had to prove to others that I could be a success, no matter the cost to myself emotionally. If it meant drinking, cheating, or not allowing others to know the real me, I would do what I had to in order to survive socially and emotionally.

10. *Organized* -- Throughout my life, I would become highly organized one day and highly disorganized the next. I have solved this problem by getting color coded files, a calendar, and a daily routine that I do over and over again. I designated places to keep my billfold, keys, and glasses. I have saved hours of looking for items by designating special places to put them. Ask my wife, Lisa! Organization is a constant challenge for me. I have also learned to multi-task in a positive manner, and this has helped with my organizational skills.

11. *Medicating myself* -- I drank too much alcohol, smoked pot, and ate too much. All these things I did to make myself feel better; however, they only made things worse for me socially, physically, and spiritually. They were temporary fixes at best. Exercising, God, and diet helped me to do away with this problem!

12. *Forgetful* --I constantly forgot where I put my important papers, billfold, keys, glasses, etc. Purchasing labels and labeling drawers helped me in many cases. I also slowed down my pace and took a deep breath and tried not to be in a hurry.

13. *Stubborn* -- If things did not go my way, I would pout as a youngster. Whenever I failed, I would be stubborn to learn what I needed to know to eventually be a success. Stubbornness can be positive and negative. Determination and resilience are good parts of being stubborn!

14. *Problems with taking my creative ideas and not putting them to good use* -- I come up with creative ideas in the shower and while exercising; I write them down and begin to work on the ideas. Would you like me to show you how many times I have written down something and not acted on it? I could write a single book on the topic of "follow-through"!

    I have learned to outline my ideas and establish time limits on completing them and putting them into action. By creating an action plan, I have actualized some of my dreams. For example, I ran two marathons and now I am completing this book by taking action, not just putting ideas down and forgetting about them.

15. *Hyper-focusing* --This is a double-edged sword; it helped me get some tasks done quickly and efficiently, yet when I get hyper-focused in my internal world, I miss out on what is being taught or talked about in social situations.

16. *Underachievement* -- This was particularly notable in my elementary through high school years. Teachers and fellow students thought I was lazy and unmotivated. I just did not know how to go about doing things the right way; my frustration tolerance was exceptionally low. Failure upon failure contributed to my underachievement.

17. *Interrupting people* -- Many times, I will get bored if people ramble on and are into their own egos. I will shut down by walking away, thinking of something different in my mind, and losing focus on the conversation. My brain is working so fast that I appear to be rude; I need to slow down and allow the other person time to speak. It is almost like I know what the person is going to say before they get to their main point in the conversation.

18. *Desiring to save the world* -- As a person with ADHD, I am compassionate and have an intuitive feel for humans. If I could, I would save the world and help everyone. It becomes a problem for me when I completely hyper-focus on the overwhelming problems of the world and ruminate about these problems; there is no way I can rescue the world! I have to start with myself and be pragmatic about who I am and how I relate to a changing world!

19. *"Pulling other people's strings"*-- At times, I would try to "get others to react" by saying things to provoke them to think and act in a certain way. At times, this was a good trait; however, it can be bad if I do not think about how it will affect the feelings of others.

20. *Sensitive to touch* -- To me, this is not a negative characteristic, but a positive one; over the years I yearned to be touched by others and feel that I was accepted. I came from a family that did not touch and embrace. Touching and loving is good for the immune system; it makes us healthy. I try to get many hugs a day! I am so happy that I have three dogs that I can pet and talk to on a daily basis; I love furry hugs!

21. *Sense of humor* -- My friends and colleagues tell me that I have a good sense of humor; I can make people laugh easily. I enjoy teaching through humor; humor has helped me in healing my ADHD symptoms. I laugh in a healthy way at myself at the silly things that I do as an ADHD individual.

22. *"Partly cloudy"*-- At times, I recall things quickly and from many years past; at other times, my brain becomes partly cloudy and fog takes over!

23. *Independent* -- I like to be independent, and that is one trait

that helps me as a teacher, husband and dad. My autonomy allows me to use my unique ADHD traits and apply them with my "out of box" thinking style.

24. *Uncoordinated* -- When I was young, I was very uncoordinated and walked like Big Bird. I tripped and dropped things, spilled milk, and bumped into furniture on a frequent basis. My inattention and cloudy thinking, I believe, added to my uncoordinated ways, as well as my physical and biological makeup.

25. *"Dancing crossed legs"*-- Whenever I got nervous while I was sitting down, my legs would dangle and dance to the nervous songs being played in my head; they would go up and down and sometimes around and around. "Hey, do you want to dance?"

26. *Highly intuitive* -- I have the ability to read people like a book by their physical expressions and my sixth sense of knowing! This can be good and bad. However, as a teacher, this helped me out tremendously in the classroom.

27. *Poor ability to give myself credit; poor self-concept* --I have dealt with this issue all my life, this was due largely to my many failures and undiagnosed ADHD. Today, I feel very good about the person I am. It has taken medicine, therapy, exercise, diet, and faith in Jesus Christ to help me become more self-actualized.

28. *Watching too much TV* -- I would get involved in watching TV, and this added to my negativity problems. Most of the channels on TV promote nothing but negative thinking. Watch out: this is fertilizer for depression and anxiety!

29. *Poor diet* -- I craved sugar; in turn, this added to my melancholy. I consumed sugar a great deal most of my life, adding to my problems of ADHD. I got high from sugar, and then, the bottom would drop out!

30. *Lack of exercise* -- When I did not exercise and eat right, this aggravated my ADHD symptoms and traits. Today, I exercise on a daily basis and eat correctly; what a difference it makes! It is just as important as taking Prozac on a daily basis.

31. *PTSD* -- I was constantly in fear and anxiety because of my

near-death experiences. I flashed back and played the events that I experienced over and over in my mind. The four near-death experiences created anxiety and fear in my life.

The traits and disorders I listed have been a part of my personality for years. I have used the positive ones to help with negative traits that needed to be addressed. The key is to recognize both your good and bad traits before they become disorders which interrupt your life economically, physically, socially, and spiritually. With persistence, patience, and just being you, you will discover that ADHD can be a good thing to have in a rapidly changing world! Remember, we can see the world differently, and that is good!

100 POSITIVE SUGGESTIONS FOR ADHD PEOPLE

As a teacher of Special and "regular" education, I have thirty-one years of expertise in teaching ADHD students, both in regular educational settings and in self-contained structured settings. I studied many subjects in graduate school and beyond, which assisted me in generating the list of one hundred positive actions an ADHD person can take. My greatest education is that I am ADHD myself; I have read widely and learned a great deal about my ADHD traits and disorders. I trust you can use the information that I used in my journey with ADHD to your advantage; pick the one(s) that will help you out in your journey in life with ADHD.

1.   *Don't consume alcohol or take drugs* -- Medicating yourself is only a temporary fix; your depression and anxiety will only get worse. Seek help from professionals if you feel anxious and depressed; the key measurement is how frequently you are depressed and how intense those feelings are. Psychological counseling and drug therapy prescribed by a child psychiatrist can help you out!

2.   *Exercise daily* -- This helps the chemistry of your brain and body; this is your natural Prozac! Pick a time that is suited

for your schedule to work out; do it for at least thirty minutes a day.

3. *Eat the basic food groups and a variety of fruits and vegetables* -- Eat healthy, and start out with protein in the morning, rather than carbohydrates. Consume small healthy meals throughout the day, as this will maintain your blood sugar level. Try to eat a variety of fruits and vegetables; this helps you maintain the vitamins you need daily, and you will not get bored with eating.

4. *Vitamins* -- I take a multi-vitamin, B-12, B-3, C, Omega 3, B Complex, and E. These vitamins promote a healthy mind and body.

5. *Eat breakfast* -- Do not leave out breakfast; this will throw your blood sugar off and fog your thinking. Be sure to include proteins, high fiber, juice; again, if you start out with carbohydrates, they will only give you an initial high and the sugar will take you spiraling down in your mood and will affect your relationships with others.

6. *Immerse yourself in literature about ADHD* -- Read many books by experts on your disorder. Read literature published by Dr. Edward M. Hallowell and Dr. John J. Ratey; they are the best in the field! Do not only read the material -- apply it to your life! Your disorder, for the most part, will not go away, but you can learn how to use it to your advantage in life, and live a quality lifestyle.

7. *Learn how you learn best* – Get to know the different techniques with which you learn best educationally. Select from concept-mapping, traditional outlining, using tape recorders, note cards, and your computer. Incorporate your positive traits with the learning styles that will aid you. Do not worry about how others learn; we all process and acquire information differently. There is one unique you!

8. *Perseverations* -- When you find yourself chasing ideas and concepts around in your mind like a 45 rpm, put a mental stop sign or detour sign in your brain. Take a deep breath and refocus your mind. You are also capable of using positive affirmations in helping cure the "circle of unwanted thoughts

and feelings."

9.   *Create small successes in your goal planning* -- Most ADHDers have experienced frequent failures. By creating "not so challenging goals," you will create a good self-image. As you win one victory after another, you can establish more difficult goals! For example, you could have a goal to run one mile without stopping. Just do not go out and try to run a mile without establishing shorter distances! You will likely quit and complain of sore muscles. First run a quarter of a mile, walk a quarter of a mile, run a quarter of a mile and then walk the last quarter; work daily at running that full mile.

10. *Hang around positive people* -- This cannot be stressed enough; many ADHD people have been battered physically and emotionally. Hang around people who feel good about who they are as humans. Success breeds success in life. Stay away from people who exhibit negative traits; they will only pull you down physically, mentally, and spiritually.

11. *Join a church* -- Take God as your main mentor in life; read scripture daily and practice what the Manual of Life, the Bible, tells you to do. Help others and become connected to a community of believers who assist others in life through outreach programs.

12. *"Get outside yourself"*-- ADHDers frequently become immersed in "self." There are others whom we can help -- thereby helping ourselves to get rid of our self-centeredness, which we use as a protective device. Join organizations such as the Red Cross or other volunteer groups in your community. You will be investing your time and talents to others in a loving way.

13. *Random acts of kindness* -- I find that by doing random acts of kindness my mood is immediately elevated, and I am being Christ-like. Open doors for others, mow your neighbor's grass (don't smoke it), visit a nursing home, and just smile at others!

14. *Listen to classical music* -- I listen to Mozart and music of other classical composers and it relaxes me. I am listening to

classical music as I type my book. It lightens me up and promotes "my flow" as a writer. The calming effect of the music is wonderful and helps my whole body-mind relationship.

15. *Daily prayer* -- Many people say they do not have time to pray, that their schedule is too busy. How can you be too busy for a God that made you and is within you? I start out every day reading scripture and praying. God does answer my prayers; but only in His time. For me, the Bible has been the key for helping me overcome my addictions and social problems. If you have tried all other avenues and still feel empty, I recommend the Bible and Jesus Christ. Study such people in the Bible as John, David, Saul, and Moses; see how they overcame their difficult life situations. God does care, if you only give Him a chance.

16. *Learn to clearly communicate* -- This is one problem I had for many years. Communication involves so many avenues. Learning to talk your problems out means reaching out when you need help. The emotions of guilt, anger, frustration, and anxiety will eat you alive. Connect with people you trust and respect.

17. *Chew gum or suck on a mint when you are nervous* -- Research has shown that chewing gum has a calming effect; in addition, taking a strong mint when you take an exam can help you think clearly!

18. *Autobiographies and biographies* -- Read about others who have experienced success in life and who have overcome difficulties; there are many people who have overcome great obstacles. Take from these people their positive suggestions, and incorporate them into your own life!

19. *A balanced life* -- This is easier said than done. Try to balance your career, family, and social life. You must take time for yourself to be able to give in healthy ways to others.

20. *Define the traits that have to change* -- Take a special notebook and graph paper, and chart your undesired behaviors; keep track of the frequency and duration of the negative behaviors that you want to change. Build in a reward system when you finally master a negative behavior. You also might

notice the intensity of your behaviors.

21. *Affirmations* -- Use positive affirmations throughout the day and before you go to bed in the evening. Your mind will recall and create new neural pathways, and learning will take place. Before you go to bed at night, recite twenty or thirty times the behavior you want to change, such as, "I am lovable and acceptable to myself," or "I will eat less tomorrow."

22. *Positive movies* -- View movies that concern challenges and are positive in nature, that illustrate how people overcome obstacles and reach their goals. Stay away from negative or violent movies that add to your woes. ADHD people have absorbed enough negative behaviors to last us literally a lifetime.

23. *Write letters* --Take time to write to those in prisons, nursing homes, or in military hospitals. Encourage others that there is hope, and love; remember to give away love that you have been given by others; be sure to love yourself first! You cannot give away love you do not have!

24. *Daily schedule* -- Write out a daily schedule the night before; get structure involved in your life! Be sure to do the items on the list you compile. Making the list will be easy; carrying the items out will be the most difficult part! You may wish to prioritize the items and give estimated times on completing them.

25. *Take a vacation* -- Taking a vacation rejuvenates you and provides a fresh outlook on your life. It is just plain healthy to get away and celebrate life. Many say they do not have the time or money to take trips, yet they gamble and buy expensive cars and clothes. A sound life is built on sound priorities and carrying them out.

26. *Massage therapy* -- Get a good massage once a month; I do this, and it is a wonderful treat. It is one of the best ways to say to you, "I like me." Exercising, eating right, and massage therapy are good friends of mine!

27. *Be kind to yourself* --Do not talk negatively to yourself; it only destroys your self-image and drags you down into depression and despair. When you make an error, do not beat

yourself up; reflect on the good times that you've experienced successes.

28. *Risk* -- Two or three times a month, try to do something that you have never done. It does not have to be a major thing that costs a lot of money. It could be as simple as traveling a different route to work, taking up yoga, eating something different and healthy for lunch, or running instead of walking. We ADDers are good at risk taking.

29. *Poetry* -- Poetry has been an excellent helper for my ADHD. I can write my inner thoughts and reflect what I am writing. There is no such thing as a bad poem in your journal. You own all of your thoughts, emotions, and attitudes. We are all authors of our own lives and carry our unique abilities with us daily in the world. Eventually you may desire to share poetry with the ones you love. During therapy, I wrote poems about certain issues and discussed them with my psychologists.

30. *Walk your dog daily* -- Become a better friend with your dog, and walk her daily. You both will be getting exercise and establishing connections with your neighbors whom you talk to on your way. Human connections are so vital in our daily lives. Just do not sit in the house!

31. *Sundae* -- As a reward, enjoy a hot fudge sundae with whipped cream once a month! I love this idea, I will be right back!

32. *Adopt a road* -- Pick up trash, you can take the cans you find to a recycling center and get money for them! You are doing your job in helping keep the earth green.

33. *Find a hobby* -- Find an activity that you would enjoy doing that would help you focus and get into the moment! Knitting, painting, rebuilding cars, building models, or playing a musical instrument.

34. *Take a warm bath* -- Before bed at night or after a long day at work, take a warm bath and put on some easy listening music. Meditate while you are in the bathtub. After a warm bath, have a cup of hot tea.

35. *Laugh and laugh more* -- "Laughter is good medicine." Rent funny movies or read the comics. Your brain will love that

you are giving it a way to relax and produce its own natural medicine! Celebrate joy. Take time with the special person in your life. Go for a walk or a bike ride. Make dinner. Have a glass of wine. Light a candle.

36. *Observe and "suck in" all of nature* -- Go out for a walk in any season of the year. Get immersed in the "now" moment of that season. Enjoy the flowers, birds, trees, snow, and special features of the land. Pray or meditate and take a few deep breaths; be sure you close your eyes and visualize peace while meditating for at least three minutes.

37. *Run through a sprinkler* -- On a hot summer day, dash through a sprinkler and get in touch with your inner child again. Be crazy and love that child that is still a part of the real you!

38. *Mellow out in the sun* -- The sun can be healthy for you; get that extra vitamin D. The sun helps depression. Listen to the birds sing, the wind blow, and feel nature's breezes. Ah, life is good!

39. *Verilux* -- Purchase a Verilux, a bright light, to help you with SAD or depression. I use this every morning for at least one hour.

40. *Watch a rainbow* -- I have chased enough rainbows; now I take time to watch the beautiful colors after the storm. Kind of like life, "There are rainbows after storms." Imagine one of your goals at the end of the rainbow that you will reach... ah, I love rainbows.

41. *Wisdom seeker* -- Seek wisdom in all her glory; read about it in the Bible and apply it to your life; it will make a big difference. Wisdom is learning to apply what you learn to life situations. There are several ways that you may learn about wisdom. Go to nursing homes, observe a newborn child, watch children playing, and talk to those who have experienced similar things that you have been going through. I invite you to join my wisdom hunter club!

42. *Smile* -- I have mentioned this before, but smiling is so critical in developing and sustaining connected in life! I recall times that I was down in the dumps and someone smiled at me -- and wow, I felt better! Giving away love makes the

world a better place.

43. *Angels* -- Know that you have a guardian angel. Someone is watching you and wanting to help you!

44. *Turn things over to God* -- God has broad shoulders; He will guide you through difficult times if you allow Him to do so. God will place people in your life to assist you on an exciting journey that only you and God only know about!

45. *Small projects around the house* -- Get involved in setting up small projects around the house; be sure to finish one before you start another! Success breeds success; and you will feel a sense of accomplishment.

46. *Enlist help from others, we are not experts in everything* -- Ask others who may have expertise in a certain area to help you out. You may have knowledge in an area that someone else needs; you can exchange ideas. Delegation is an art; it is not a weakness!

47. *Build a key rack* -- I forget where I put my keys, so I purchased a key rack and put it by the doors; it helps my sanity by keeping me from looking around an hour for my keys! Make sure the rack is in a visible place.

48. *Color code files* -- Color code your files with your favorite colors; have the different colors be symbolic for the different months of the year, for example. I know I have mentioned this before!

49. *Count to three* --After coming into home from work, immediately go to a quiet place for five minutes and meditate. This will help you to relax. Then, go put your items away such as your keys, pocket change, and clothes. Take time to place the items where you have designated them to go.

50. *Recorder* -- Purchase a recorder to help remind you of your daily tasks; go put daily affirmations on the recorder to help you in changing behaviors that you deem inappropriate.

51. *Vocabulary* -- Get a notebook, and keep a list of a new word that you look up every day, or you can make a journal and put it on your PC. Adding a word every day will increase your vocabulary!

52. *Don't be critical of yourself* -- Ask others to make suggestions

about solving problems which may help in improving communication with them if needed. For example, I used to try to talk with my wife, Lisa, constantly while she was in another room and she could not hear me. She purchased walkie-talkies. Our communication skills immediately improved. "What did you say?" comments would no longer be heard!

53. *Forgive* --Empty your closet of emotions that are bothering you and hanging around. Your health will improve, and your love for others will improve. Burn them in the fireplace!

54. *Get a haircut or facial* -- Be kind to yourself and get groomed up! It makes you feel fresh and adds to the positive self-image you are working on!

55. *Clean your closet* -- Go through your clothes and give away the ones that are no longer needed. Take the items to a local charity. You will feel good about helping others, and will discover that life is not all about clothes in the closet. Be sure to check pockets for money!

56. *Work clothes* -- Before you start your work week, get your clothes organized so you can have them ready for each day. Iron the clothes you will be wearing. The night before, lay your clothes out, so in the morning you can easily find them!

57. *Checklist* -- Before you travel, make a checklist of the things you will need. Consider the number of days you will be staying and plan accordingly. When I have not planned correctly, I have ended up taking too much and dragging another bag along which I did not have to take!

58. *Your wallet* -- When you travel, you can buy a special belt or passport holder in which to put your important documents. Be sure to put all important items in one place; if you place them here and there, you will take unneeded time in trying to find them.

59. *Social groups* -- When you go to a party or a social gathering, listen to others and give them a chance to speak. Do not interrupt conversations that others are having. We ADHDers are good at interrupting -- I know that I am!

60. *Body proximity* -- While in a conversation; do not get into

someone else's comfort zone. Allow three to four feet when you are standing and talking to them. No one enjoys being crowded.

61. *Speaking* -- Learn to have a limit on the amount of time you talk and give the other person a chance to answer your questions or speak back. Be positive in your conversations, and relax!

62. *Be complimentary* -- Do not feign emotions; be genuine, and learn to compliment people about their dress, any successes, or nice things they have done for you or someone else. Connecting with others positively will help your friendships grow.

63. *Appointments*-- Make a plan where to put your appointments; do not have commitments on your Palm and others in two or three different calendars!

64. *When driving* -- We ADHDers are inclined to be impatient on the roads and drive fast when we become frustrated. When someone makes you angry, count to three and pull over or park and take a deep breath. It is well worth the effort; conflict and lawsuits are not good.

65. *Persistent* -- "Never, never, never, give up." This was stated by the great Vince Lombardi of the Green Bay Packers. When trying to alter a negative behavior, it takes a lot of effort before the behavior is permanently imprinted in our minds. Think of the hundreds of times we have emitted some undesired behaviors -- in some cases, it's been years. We must create new neurological pathways before the new actions can be done on a regular basis.

66. *Communication and tone of voice* -- When giving suggestions or having disagreements with others, be aware of the inflection in your voice. Be calm and do not be sardonic when disagreeing with others. Often people are not aware of how they are saying something, especially in a heated discussion.

67. *Be a social butterfly* -- At social gatherings, become a social butterfly and do not get locked into one conversation all night long! Floating around will help you connect with many individuals.

68. *If you have spelling problems* -- Read voraciously about your problem and work on it daily. Today we have spell check that helps me out on the computer, yet I carry a small dictionary with me when I think I may need it. In today's technological world, we can carry our PDAs or other gadgets with us and use them as a reference.

69. *Quaint and quiet place* -- When the hustle and bustle of the world is dragging me down, I like to go to my "secret quiet place." I need time to refocus, listen to the quiet and pray. Near my home is a park where I go and talk with God -- it is refreshing to refocus and embrace life.

70. *Names* --Before you go to important events, try to recall the names of people who are going to be at the occasion. We all like to be remembered; this makes us feel loved and worthy. If you can recall something positive about a person, mention that in conversation.

71. *Emotional frame of mind* -- The reason that you may not be learning something may be because you need to resolve emotional issues. Try to clear your mind as much as possible and get the "cobwebs" out. It is so hard to learn anything when our minds are not focused.

72. *"The little guy on my shoulder"* -- I have created a little helper with a quiet soothing voice on my shoulder to help me out in times of distress. I call him "the little dude on my shoulder." At times when I am making major decisions, I like to consult with this man, who is very objective, and talks with me about all options I should consider.

73. *Role models* -- I encourage you to adopt role models in your life that you can take positive traits from and incorporate them into your personality. These role models' attributes can help us develop into better humans. My favorite role model is Ron Santo, the old Cub, who has fought diabetes for many years. Ron has gone through such tremendous physical and mental pain in his life. Ron lost both of his legs, yet remains healthy with his positive attitude and love for life. He has raised millions of dollars for the Diabetes Foundation.

74. *Toxic worry and fact* -- If there is a predicament do not sit and

ruminate about the problem; it will only make your health worse. Address the issue(s) that are bothering you.

75. *Awards* --As you achieve your small and large goals, be sure you put reminders in a place where you can visually observe them. There are times when you may get a ribbon or certificate as an award. Proudly take the awards and display them where you can view them. It is not boasting when you take such action; it only reminds you all of the hard work you have devoted to a project.

76. *Motivating quotes* -- I take inspirational quotes and display them where I can memorize them and then implement!

77. *Hasty decisions* -- Before you make any big decisions, allow time to pass, and reflect on the positive and negative consequences of your choices the best as you can. We cannot control all the consequences, yet we can be wise in decision making based on what we know is true. I am good at looking at the whole picture!

78. *How to forget the past* --There are many ways we can clear our minds of the past. I have written my hurts on a piece of paper and burned them in the fireplace. I would create my own unique rituals of saying goodbye and burning the paper. I also enjoy going by the ocean, and when a wave comes to shore, giving my problems to that wave to take it out over the vast ocean to never be seen again!

79. *Life is too short* -- Remember, "today is the first day of the rest of your life."

80. *Trust your sixth sense* -- One of the major positives us ADHDers have is our strong intuition. Learn to trust your gut feeling; most of the time, your feelings will be correct.

81. *"To thine own self be true"*—Being honest with what you must change can be very difficult, yet liberating.

82. *Be aggressive with change*—If you put off a negative behavior or trait that needs to be addressed, it only will pull you down more! Be assertive, talk with God, and have confidence in yourself that you can and will change for the better in your life.

83. *Generosity* -- Many attention deficit disordered individuals

are generous to a fault; the end result is that people can and will take advantage of this gift. Know that it is not only money you can give, but your time.

84.   *When reading books* -- When reading books ,take notes that you can apply to your life and do it!

85.   *Meetings* -- Bring a tape recorder to staff meetings; I got bored when I attended meetings at school. I simply turned on a tape recorder to make sure I did not miss what I was not listening to. By the way, I wrote some of my best poetry during these meetings !

86.   *Family history* -- Be aware of your family history as far as health related genetics; you can do your best through diet, exercise, and medication to help you to be the best you can.

87.   *Watch the caffeine* --This is so important; late in the day, especially. If you drink too much coffee or pop in the afternoon, you will have difficulty sleeping.

88.   *Drink lots of water* -- In order to make our brain and body work well we need lots of water. Our brain is made up of around 80% of water. Every day, drink at least eight glasses of water. Remember too that fruits and veggies are high-water-content foods, and are healthy for you!

89.   *Take good notes-* While reading or in seminars, take good notes that you can use to become a better person. When the note taking is done, go home and make a list of the important things you can use and try to apply them accordingly to your daily life.

90.   *Continuing education* -- Education should be a lifelong endeavor; continue studying subject matter that relates to your field or expertise. In addition, take courses that you want to know more about in life, but have not taken time to do so.

91.   *Psychotherapy* -- Do not be frightened to go to counseling whenever you need to; life constantly changes, and so do we.

92.   *Stare at the full moon* -- When I get uptight, I love going out on my deck and meditating with the moon. Ah, just wondering how it hangs up in the sky is amazing to me.

93.   *Adjustment of medication* -- Do not be afraid of adjusting

your medication when necessary; you may have to for different reasons.

94. *Offer to babysit your grandchildren* -- Whenever I watch my granddaughter, my troubles go away. To see how a child solves his or her problems is wonderful. You know, my granddaughter, Sophia, sometimes just walks away from a problem she cannot solve; that is not a bad idea!

95. *Have confidence* -- Keep a positive attitude, and have confidence to avoid toxic worry. Whenever we feel that we are vulnerable, we are giving ourselves less power and therefore increased worrying. Know that you are special, and have confidence that God will guide you.

96. *Structure your life* -- Be sure to add structure to your life. Plan your retirement, have a cash reserve fund, and plan your funeral; these things will put your mind at rest and allow you to concentrate more on the magical moments in life.

97. *"Big boys do cry"* -- Despite what the "Four Seasons" used to sing -- men, let us cry; it is healthy and productive.

98. *Memorize a Bible verse* -- Take the time to memorize a Bible verse. Write the verse on a card and post it where you can see it. Apply the verse to your life; you will see a difference.

99. *Shaking hands and eye contact* -- When shaking hands, do it lightly, and gaze into the other person's eyes with respect.

100. *Be the self you know* -- "I am who I am because 'I am,' and this is good enough for me, you are you and I am me, let us both celebrate and both be free!"

I hope that you, the reader, may benefit from any of the items on the list that you feel to be beneficial. As you read widely, come up with your own ideas about how you can become healthy and productive. I wish you the best in your journey with ADHD; in many ways, it has been a blessing to me more than a curse!

ADHD COACHING AND MENTORING

An ADHD coach can help you with your ADHD. Below, I share with you what an ADHD coach does and what the process entails;

ADHD coaching is another option in helping you to become a self-actualized individual.

ADHD mentoring or coaching is an ongoing process which focuses on the client taking action toward his or her goals, desires, or in actualizing their dreams. The process of inquiring or questioning is applied by the coach; the ADHD mentor stresses ways for an individual to use their talents and strengths to the utmost. The coach shows the client how to function with their disability. In addition, the mentor trains the client how to be accountable for his or her actions. The three basic goals of an ADHD coach are to provide a client with:

1. Support
2. Structure
3. Strategies

Do all people who have ADHD require a coach? The answer is no; however, many should inquire about getting a mentor if their lives are not progressing in the direction they desire. After getting a medical evaluation, immerse yourself in literature, surround yourself with positive people, and get counseling. After that, we may, however, desire to get a coach to encourage and to be our lighthouse. Coaches can give advice and offer suggestions that we may not have thought of using in reaching our desired goals.

Many ask if the ADHD coach is a certified therapist; the answer is no. The coach works with the ADHD individual to establish realistic short and long term goals; he or she will show the client how to go about reaching the desired outcomes. In contrast, a therapist helps with emotional problems and growth.

Anyone who desires to help another person can be an ADHD coach! Some say it should not be your spouse; however, my wife mentors me in many areas of my life. It may be dangerous having a spouse as a coach; they are sometimes too close to the situation and cannot remain objective. The important thing is that there is trust between the coach and the client. "Game playing" is not allowed and can be dangerous to a client's health. Honesty and integrity must exist if a client wants to get a coach and be helped.

If you want to hire an ADHD coach, the cost varies according to the coach's expertise and experience; I charge $50.00 an hour to coach a client. The coach and potential client arrange schedules through e-mail, phone, and setting up appointments face to face when necessary. You can discuss with your coach the methods that you desire to use.

You may wonder what the relationship between psychotherapy and coaching is. Coaching may be used concurrently with psycho-therapeutic work. It should not be used as a substitute; psychothera-pists have advanced degrees and are experts in their chosen fields. A coach may offer certain advice or suggestions during the coaching process; it is up to the client to determine if he or she should use the advice given by the coach. The client must take the ultimate re-sponsibility for choices to be made. I have a Master's of Science in Education/Special Education, and I have training in behavior modi-fication and goal-setting techniques; in addition, I have knowledge in tutoring clients in selected academic areas if they prefer to include that in our coaching-client relationship.

As a trainer, I ask my clients to make adjustments toward goals they are trying to obtain. By modifying certain goals, the client can reach their desired objective. As a coach, I do not remediate behav-iors of my client; this should be done through therapy with a psy-chiatrist or psychologist. It is not a coach's purpose to understand a client's past behaviors. I would like to point out again that expertise or advanced degrees may or may not be present in the coach's cre-dentials. I have certifications in several areas of learning; therefore, I offer learning methods acquired while receiving my undergradu-ate and graduate degrees. Like most coaches, I use my credentials to facilitate the coaching and client process. I will not apply my knowledge to diagnose, direct, or design major life solutions for my client. I may, however, recommend a client for help if he or she asks me to do so. My background in Sociology-Anthropology, minor in social work, and study of psychology all aid me in my relationship with my clients.

At the beginning of coaching, I give an inventory of the multiple-intelligences to ascertain what the client's strengths and weaknesses are in given areas. This aids me in getting to know the client much better. The information that I gather from the client is to help the client to become aware of his or her goals and to stay on a course of action. A written statement is signed by both the client and myself if he or she desires the information to be shared with a therapist.

As a coach, I address a wide variety of personal and professional topics. With every client, I talk about the scope and depth of the route we desire to establish, pertaining to goal setting and attainment. I hope that, by coaching, I can leave my client with a greater sense of self and the ability to establish short and long range goals by making them through their own choices. We are all uniquely different, and what may work for one client may not be effective for another. As a mentor and coach, I am interested in each person's learning styles and how they carry out that knowledge to others.

Being coached is not a lifelong process. Hopefully the client will reach goals and learn better how to establish them; the end result will be leading a productive and healthy life. Once the client becomes honest with themselves and can see the positive changes they are making in their lives, a coach may be no longer be required.

Below is an inventory titled, "Are you Ready to be Coached?" Look at the questions, and see if you are ready to be mentored. Many people who have ADHD are not ready to hire a coach right away, or maybe not ever. I believe when an individual wants to bring about healthy change in their lives they will do it at any cost; it is then time to hire a coach.

The family, friends, and co-workers of an ADHD person may want him or her to modify their behaviors right away. However, the ultimate responsibility lies with the person needing the help. Anyone who desires to change for the better must have the intrinsic yearning to take the steps on their own. Without the determination of wanting to change, failure will only be lurking around the corner!

"Are You Ready To Be Coached?"

1. I am reliable and will be on time for appointments and calls.
   1 2 3 4

2. I will allow the coach to "coach," and I will do all the work which is required of me.
   1 2 3 4

3. I will keep my word and try to be true to myself, my family, and goals.
   1 2 3 4

4. I am open to change in my life, and this is the correct time for me to go into a coaching relationship.
   1 2 3 4

5. I will be open and trusting, allowing the coach to "present new ways" of doing things, if necessary.
   1 2 3 4

6. I will have integrity and be honest with myself and the coach.
   1 2 3 4

7. If I find that I am not relating to the coach, I will tell him or her as soon as possible so I can build a trusting relationship with the coach and any necessary modifications can be made.
   1 2 3 4

8. I will stop the self-defeating behaviors which have limited my success in reaching my goals.
   1 2 3 4

9. Change is important in my life, and I possess the adequate amount of funds; I know that coaching is one of the best investments I can make in my life financially and emotionally.

      1 2 3 4

10. I am an individual who can share the credit and success with my coach and mentor; we can work as a team.

      1 2 3 4

Now add up the numbers that you put a square around and get a total score _____

10-20 _____ I am not coachable at the present time.
21-30 _____ I am coachable; I will honor the rules my coach makes.
31-40 _____ I am coachable and will change.
41-50 _____ I am very coachable and am willing to be coached.

CHAPTER THREE

BABY BOOMER'S ADHD POEMS

Poetry has been a healthy and creative outlet for me throughout my life. It has been through poetry that I have been able to share my positive self and motivate others. I would like to share some of the ADHD poems that I have written about myself. Back in the 1950s and 1960s we did not recognize that ADHD existed. Today, education has come a long way in identifying and dealing with ADHD in both youngsters and adults. Typically, there are eighteen symptoms listed in the DSM-IV, the diagnostic manual of mental problems.

At this moment, as I have previously stated, there are around eight to ten million adults in the US around with ADHD traits or disorders: anxiety, depression, not completing tasks on time, constantly interrupting people, not being able to finish tasks, broken promises, and the core symptoms of restlessness, impulsivity, and distractibility.

Through my poetry, I share with you about my feelings about ADHD; you will learn about the many traits and disorders I have dealt with for sixty-two years. I have come a long way in dealing with the various issues. Just being aware that I have ADHD helped me tremendously in making adjustments in my life. "Today is the first day of the rest my life," is a quote that I read on a wall written while I was in Vietnam; it applies to my life every day.

Comment: Many people with ADHD have trouble turning our great ideas into important actions.

AHA, I HAVE AN IDEA

Aha, I have a great idea on my mind;
This concept is one of a kind.
One day I will write a book on ADHD my unique way.
I have the chapters outlined in my mind's eye;
I hope my book will be published before I die.
My book of ideas will be presented before others;
It will help all my ADHD sisters and brothers.
Now it is ten years later; I am having the same refrain.
"One day, I will write a book on ADHD my unique way."
My ideas someday will come together;
I just have to get my mind out of this foggy weather!

Comment: Chronic underachievement is a characteristic of ADHD people.

SMART IS NOT PASSING ONE TEST

I knew that I was bright, but I just got Cs, that was not right.
I failed first grade in a flash;
I tried to do my best.
I was blind to the academic lights;
My mind swirled around and around
    left to right.
I thought different than most of the rest,
My teachers sighed as I could not pass
    a traditional test.
I was not lazy or crazy…
I just underachieved with zest.
Ask an ADDer -- he knows the best!

Comment: I was moody as a child and the people who loved me could not figure out why; neither could I. My parents, teachers, and friends frequently commented how my moods went up and down like an elevator. I was an empathetic, deep feeling, and a caring person; I did not enjoy being happy and then sad.

I SWING HIGH AND LOW

One day I would be happy, the next day sad;
I was loving and really not bad.
These feelings of my heart came and went;
I yearned to be happy, but just couldn't!
When things wouldn't go my way,
I would not want to play.
Like a swing that goes high and then low,
My moods never stopped, they were always on the go.

Comment: As an ADHDer I see life through different lenses than the "normal" person.

MY EYES ARE NOT YOURS

I view the world through a kaleidoscope of different hues.
You see the world red, I see it blue.
You remember many things, I recall few.
I study over and over for an idea to stay…
You remember the facts right away.
Let us not judge each other's hues;
For I am I and you are you.

Comment: Frequently our minds move fast and we make hasty decisions. We want to take an action right away without considering all the details. This frequently got me into trouble. It is so important to consider all the facts!

NOW PLEASE

Quick, I must buy that car now.
Hurry, I must buy that beautiful home.
Hastily, I must have the best suit!
It won't be there for me later, I will get it now.
I must get married fast, she may be the last!
I must mow the lawn before the dew is off the grass;
My mind is anxious and wants to complete the task.
Wait, I will be right back...
This revolving mind of mine must get back on track!

Comment: I have the tendency to change tasks and end up multi-tasking and forgetting some of those "multi-tasks!"

TISKET A TASKET

I am cleaning the kitchen floor,
     which I think is a fathom of a bore.
I forgot to bring the broom to do this task,
Rushing out into the garage I get the broom
     to bring back.
I see in the garage the recycling bin, it needs to be
     cleaned, so there I begin.
I get a bucket filled with water; I know that
     I am not doing what I oughter…
I pick up the broom and leave the bucket by the bin.
I zoom into the house to go where I began.
As I cross the living room floor, I see my shoes,
     clothes and much much more.
Picking them up I go into the bedroom
     to place them in a drawer and out of the room I zoom!
Now I am in a state of multi-tasking flow;
I know my mind knows not where to go.
I stop by my office and peer in the door,
     my PC is on and the electrical bill will soar.
I walk in the room and turn off the switch,
     my ADHD mind is stuck in a glitch.
I now sit at the computer which is no longer on;
I am listening to my radio which is singing a song.
As I wake up from my moment's sleep,
     I saunter down the hall and into the kitchen I go to sweep.

Comment: I sometimes hold things fast to my mind and I will not let it go. I perseverate and perseverate.

PLEASE PAUSE THE PERSEVERATION

Please put on pause the perseverations in my head.
Each day the same thoughts remain with me
    until I go to bed.
Swirling and spinning, my mind never rests;
It keeps reminding me that I failed many
    of life's tests.
Again and again and again its sounds reverberate…
Your failures are many and it is getting late.
I am exhausted from my recording mind being stuck…
I take a deep breath and put my mind on pause…
I say, "This recording of mine has no real cause!"

Comment: One of the disorders I have as an ADHDer is anxiety. I have fought with this demon since I was very young. I did not know why I was anxious, because there was not really anything major to be nervous about. To calm myself, I ate food high in sugar and drank alcohol; this, of course, made matters worse.

ANXIETY AND "I"

I feel nervous and I know not why,
      my life is good, but I year to cry and cry.
Small droplets of perspiration appear on my face;
My heart starts to pump and pump like I am running
      a race.
I am squirming and wiggling with doubt and fear,
      I want to take a gulp of beer.
Ah, with a sip I feel like the rest;
You know, you "normal" people who are
      strong and always at your best!
I am drinking a beer just to make a tweak;
      I can now be free to be the real me.
I am now a lot like you,
      we both can see through the same kind
          of hues.
Wait, my logic is wrong, I am singing
      the wrong type song.
The day after I awake from my beer bash…
I am depressed, anxious, and not at all
      at rest.
I stop and peer within my restless heart.
I am back to square one; that is the sad part.
Anxiety and I never did part!

Comment: When I was in first and second grade, it was difficult for me to read because of my ADHD and learning disability.

DICK AND JANE

When I was in elementary school we read
    Dick and Jane;
I reversed the letters when I read and this
    created pain.
The members of my class would laugh and scoff;
They would point their fingers at me
    telling me that I did not know a lot.
This refrain I heard from my teacher again and again;
"Please read slower and read it again."
My mind was in reverse and did not have
    a forward gear.
The only words I read involved fear.
Panicking that I would make a mistake;
Others would laugh and I took a double take…Shame.

Comments: I sought high stimulations in my life through sports, risky behaviors, and alcohol abuse; as a child I liked to jump off high places and pretend I was a parachuting out of an airplane.

JUMPING JACK FROM HIGH

As a child I liked to swing high,
I would sit in my pretend airplane
      and fly her up into the calm blue sky.
I am a fighter pilot zooming without care;
I feel free without any despair.
As I pump high to the top of my swing,
I would bail out over the playground,
      creating a scene.
I would land on my rear and get such a big rush;
      by bailing out high and landing on my tush.

Comment: I have the tendency to change subjects quickly when I am talking to another person; ask my wife, Lisa! At times, when she is in the middle of a sentence, my mind is off on another thought! It ends up that I cover myriad topics within five minutes. However, this is rude to the person to whom I am talking; ask my wife!

THE WEATHER

My wife talks about the weather;
I interrupt her and compliment her on her sweater.
She tells me thank you and before she talks again…
I say that we should go on a swim.
"A great idea," she replies quickly.
Before she goes on, I say, "Your hands are sticky?"
Again she tries to reply as fast as she can,
Before she elaborates, I am on another subject again.
My big mouth appears kind of rude;
My ADHD behavior thinks it is shrewd…
I cover ten topics in a minute or two;
However, I remember there are me and you.
I ask, "What did you say? My mind is out of skew."

Comment: I use a calendar to put important dates on so I may keep an organized daily schedule. There is one problem -- I tend to lose the calendar and buy another and another!

NO WONDER I CAN'T GET A DATE

I trot to the store and buy a calendar to get organized,
      I take it home and write on it to prioritize.
Tossing the calendar on my desk;
Into the bedroom I go to rest.
When I get up I peer into my dresser drawers,
      I find a pocket calendar which I begin to explore.
Having two calendars does not seem that bad,
      how can I miss appointments that I have?
I put appointment dates on the many squares
      with colorful pens;
I do this on both calendars over and over again.
As the week passes, I cannot recall
      where I placed both of my calendars,
         they are not on my desk wall!
I must go to the store and buy
      just one more to hang on my office door.
I cannot take the time to continue to explore…
I purchased one calendar to place dates on again.
After I post the events one more time,
      I toss away the calendars;
         I have the dates in my mind

Comments: Many ADHDers think that because they have ADHD traits or disorders, their lives are doomed. Quite to the contrary, our lives are filled with excitement, creativity, and adventure. We learn to adapt to the world in our own unique thinking styles. "We" are special!

"WE"

We are highly intuitive people who can read others like a book;
We think out of the box and persistently look!
We peer for answers when others stop;
We have resilience while others do not.
When people say you can't do it that way,
We just laugh and invent our own concepts to stay.
Sensitive, warm, and empathetic too;
The friends we make are true blue.
We know the original from the fake;
We are zany and crazy, this is not a mistake.
Just ask the boring ones who we are...
They will say "flaky,"
We will say a star!

Comment: I have been called lazy, unmotivated, and a person who would not pay attention in the classroom. Through grade school and middle school I got only Cs. In high school, I began to get a few Bs and Cs. Later in life, when I went back to college after flunking out, I earned a B.S. and an M.S. degree with honors! Following is a narrative of what a former teacher told me in church one day-- how he viewed me when I was his student in middle school years earlier. He was not mean about what he said; it was just the time we were in, back in the 50s and 60s...I laughed at his comment!

"I" MADE IT

As I trudged through my school years
      I knew I was capable, but many sneered.
Teachers could not understand
      why they had to repeat to me time and time again.
My auditory discrimination was such an abomination.
I did not hear or read the words the teachers said;
I barely could interpret by sight; my phonetics was dead.
I tore up my papers and started over and over;
The many eraser marks made the papers look older.
I wanted to be a success, but life was getting colder;
I tried my best.
Several decades passed since those difficult reading
      and listening days when I was in a haze.
I am now a retired teacher, what am I to say?
I made it through school with determination and grit,
      I tried and tried and never said quit.
Life has its funny quirks and tests;
One day at church, I saw a former teacher, I had his class.
We talked and laughed about my junior high school days,
      and what did the kind teacher have to say?
I told him I was jealous of all the smart kids way back when,
He just gave me a smile and said with a grin,
"Weck, you were just lazy!"

Comment: As a student, I had the tendency to get lost in thought while the teacher taught. If the conversations were not stimulating, my attention would go somewhere else, even if I had to create the scene myself.

LOST IN THOUGHT

Staring out the window, I am watching the falling rain;
The teacher is talking and I am playing outside
      having fun without schoolhouse pain.
The soccer ball I kick from my foot to others,
      I would rather be outside if I had my druthers.
I am in my own world of joy and not pain;
My world of thought swirls over and over again.
The teacher's words are running into each other
      they make no sense, why go any farther?
Suddenly the classroom door slams again and again,
      I suddenly awaken from my dream world within.
I am assuming the class is not over;
Out the door I scram…
Only to repeat this scene again and again;
"Who says school is boring?"

Comment: Numerous morally incorrect labels have been given to me by former teachers, coaches, and parents of my friends. Words are like bombs, they destroy the person they are directed at; hurt and angry became a residual in my heart.

ADJECTIVES FOR AN ADHD PERSON

lazy
crazy
hazy
flaky
undisciplined
behavior problem
rude
zoned out
Yet, very gifted and no one knows;
Except the Little Prince:
"It is only with the heart that one can
        see rightly, what is essential is
                invisible to the eyes."

Comment: Focusing is both good and bad for me as an ADHDer. At times I can hyper-focus and get jobs done quickly, at other times I cannot focus and complete a task!

MY MIND IS LIKE A PAIR OF BINOCULARS

My mind can focus like binoculars;
From time to time my mind's eye is so clear and sharp.
It examines and recognizes even the smallest details.
I become aware of the small spots on a bird's wings
      or the camouflaged bird sitting in a tree.
There are times, however, why my grey matter is out of focus;
I am blind to what is around me and cannot pay
      attention to details, sounds, and my surroundings.
My thoughts and feelings are taking a vacation.
I may be processing ideas about creative endeavors
      that no one else has ever thought about.
I am blind with reality, yet alive in another colorful world
      of thoughts, dreams, inventions, and wild
         corny ideas.
I guess this is not so bad at times; only if I would act on
      all of my masterful ideas!
At other times it hurts because I miss out on all
      the "stimulating" conversations that are
         going on about me.
Binoculars are not bad…
They can focus in and out and see a wide picture
      of what is going on.
I need to be in control of my binoculars…
"Oh, what did you say?"

Comment: Did you ever get the ADHDer's blues? You know what to do, sing that song, you can't go wrong!

ADHD AND THE BLUES

Did you ever get the ADHD blues?
Your mind swirls around and around,
     Spinning like leaves upon the ground.
Did you ever wonder why your mind leaps
     hurdles and hurdles of every kind?
The rivers of emotions swirl and flow into
     your heart and your restless soul?
I say, sing the ADHD blues with all of your might,
     your feelings are yours and are just right!
The mind's rivers twist and flow;
     often I do not know where they go.
Perhaps they flow into oceans of woe.
I say yell out your unique ADHD song…
It' not wrong, not wrong, not wrong;
Sing those redundant songs…
Ya got to know that the ocean is vast
     and can take on your woeful song;
Sing those ADHD blues; this is your ADHD way!
I say, this is your ADHD way!
Your life will never be the same…
Singing your song will lift your pain.
Your life is ok, and you're not to blame.
Your life is ok, and you're not to blame!

Comment: I frequently experience "brain fog," because of the lack of functioning of my frontal lobes. I try to enhance my lobes by doing certain brain exercises and knowing my learning styles.

MY DYSFUNCTIONAL LOBES

My frontal lobes are not the best,
  they don't give my brain a rest!
My situational awareness is not present;
I need to build my muscles with effervescence!
If I know my learning style, my brain will
  get into shape and I can smile!
I play checkers and chess too;
It is painful for this right-brainer
  to enjoy and do…
Logical games are now my hobby;
I pump weights for my physical body.
Frontal lobes you can be my pal;
I must do things different to excel!
"Checkmate!"

CHAPTER FOUR

BABY BOOMER'S POEMS:
ERAS OF GOOD FEELINGS

Poetry about the eras I was growing up, during the 1950s through the 1960s, represents an important part of who I am. There were good times, bad times, and then times that "just were."

Thought: From generation to generation we all have our own special dreams, desires, and goals. To me, goals are dreams actualized; as an ADHD person, I am really a dreamer!

PORCH TIME

Those summer nights on the front porch
  we neighborhood kids would assemble
    together to have fun.
WGN and Wally Phillips' voice were our
  night friends.
As children we talked about what the future held,
  such as the impossibility of flying a man to the moon!
Our humor was free flowing and fun.
We chatted about humanity and all the potential
  that life held.
Peering into the sky, we gazed at the "old man in the moon."
We knew for sure that no one would ever reach that yellow
  crescent in the sky!
Dreams and visions do come true -- ask Neil Armstrong!

Thought: Remember the penny loafers? I use to put steel clips on the bottom. By trying to be cool, I was called into the principal's office.

LOAFERS NOT LOAFING

My penny loafers did not loaf,
    they were cool and that is no joke!
On the bottom I nailed steel clips;
They caused me strife, as I walked down the hall
    my loafers scratched the floors and made chips.
Before I knew it, I was standing at the principal's door;
The following day my clips were no more…

THOUGHT: Can you recall the outdoor games we played? Those summer nights were fun and filled with excitement!

GAMES THAT COST NO MONEY

Can you recall the toppling of tin cans?
Those days and nights we played without end?
The summer breezes of childhood days,
    came and went as we cheerfully played.
I positioned my foot upon the cylinder can
    by the old elm tree;
I counted one, two, and three.
I was looking for you and you were peering at me.
Screaming, running, and quiet times too,
    these were the days that we boomers knew…
Today the cans are tossed about;
They lie in the gutters along the highway's routes.
Our cylinders are no longer treasures;
They are just "cans"…
However, our dreams will always stay
    we will never throw them in the gutters
        to go their own way!

THOUGHT: The neighborhood candy stores will never be replaced in my mind's eye. I experienced many joyful moments; there life-long friends were made.

PENNY CANDY: DO YOU HAVE ANY CENTS?

Yum, yum, those gummy bears
    and two for one cent treats.
I saved my cents, so I could buy my sweets!
Bazooka, the pink gum, was fun to chew;
Inside, the comics I read and learned from too;
I blew bubbles and they popped in my face!
Let us not forget those dots on the paper,
You, know, that tiny hard candy with flavor?
I must not fail to remember those black sugary bears;
They never growled at me or made me scared.
The tiny bears I will always savor;
In spite of doing my dentist such a favor!

THOUGHT: The 1957 Chevy was more than a car; it was our place to kiss!

KISSING IN THE '57 CHEVY

Those years of summer dreams in the past;
We kissed our girls and thought our love would last.
We had no money and barely any gas.
The girls' pony tails streamed down their backs;
Our Chevy was the "Cadillac."
We guys wore penny loafers upon our feet,
        our clothes were groovy and kind of neat.
Butch wax of pink was plastered in our hair;
The world was ours without a care. "May I kiss you?"
That was the beginning of the end of our brief love affair!

THOUGHT: Remember the 1957 Chevy, and the well-built body and engine?

A HOT NUMBER "57"

She had a body finished with class;
     the colors were one of the best.
Roaring sounds came from her heart;
She was my lover from the start.
Her rims were shiny and clear as a mirror;
That old Chevy will always be dear;
Close to my heart and aging soul.
I say the "57" ride is my way to go!

THOUGHT: Roy Rogers was a man from whom we boomers learned some of our early childhood values.

ROY ROGERS, OUR MAN

Roy Rogers was our hero;
His smile and spirit were the real deal.
Trigger, his buddy, possessed long strides;
     as he galloped with Roy by his side.
Roy showed us through his heroic deeds
     what was right from wrong, and how to succeed.
We hearkened to his songs of hope;
This great man was no hoax.
We give our hearty thanks to Roy and Trigger,
They are always our happy neighbors.

THOUGHT: The corner candy store was the place many of us kids in the "hood" gathered to talk and slurp pop and devour candy.

AT DA CORNER STORE

Do ya recall da corner candy store?
The sodas were in glass bottles, not like cans today.
Pollution of tin cans was not filling our lands;
We got money back for returning the bottles.
Those sultry summer nights we walked
       to the store, dashing in through the entrance
          to grab a cool pop from the container.
There was Pepsi, Coke, RC, Lime Soda, and more.
We opened the glass bottle and popped off the lid;
Next we would pay for our pop and go sit
       on the front porch of the store.
I used licorice as a soda straw and added
       fizzes to my pop to make it bubble!
For seating we used the wooden pop cases that
       were empty waiting for people to return
          the glass bottles.
"This was this" and "that was that,"
       the old times at the store were the best.
Hey, ya want to go to the store?
We can talk, and much more…
At the old candy store, this is no more.

THOUGHT: Have you lost your marbles? Find them and let's take aim!

MARBLES WERE OUR AIM

Hey guys, do your recall the days when we
    took a stick and drew a circle in the dirt?
Arriving at school early, we had the
    marble bags attached to our waists.
Those colorful gems we played with and traded
    made the day so much fun,
Life was filled with joy and we had no guns…
The only shooter we had was the one
    we used to knock marbles out of our circles.
Today guns are hurtful; they kill!

THOUGHT: Every era has its unique political, social, and economic themes.

BABY BOOMERS' TIMES

The Baby Boomers' years are a time in history;
The moments in time were not a mystery.
Ball games, marbles, jump ropes, and hula hoops
    all were games that were nifty.
Year after year songs by Elvis, the Beatles, the Rolling Stones,
    Ricky Nelson, and Ray Charles told countless stories.
A whopping 76 million births came to Earth between
    1946 and 1964, the population began to soar.
The times came and went…
But Baby Boomers will always be magnificent;
The main feature of any show!

THOUGHT: Buildings are the best of friends when buddies are not around to play catch on a summer's day.

THE WALL IS MY FRIEND

When I had no friends to toss a ball,
       I went to my elementary school's walls.
The walls of the old school played catch with me,
The only rule was that I hit the wall so the ball
       would bounce back to me.
I imagine that I am Ernie Banks playing
       shortstop and fielding the elusive grounder.
My shabby glove is dangling from my left hand;
I swiftly gulp up the ball and toss it to my
       imaginary first baseman.
The sphere at times shot to my left or right;
I did not know for sure what direction the next
       bounce would take, but kept her in sight.
At times I misjudged the ball and it would roll
       by me out into the street.
As my youthful years passed, the wall and I became
       the best of friends.
The brick barrier assisted me in becoming a good baseball player.
Isn't that strange, that one of my best friends
       was the school wall?
Today as I go by the grade school, I notice the old wall
       has been knocked down.
I thought my favorite wall and school
       would never fall…
Just like people, physical structures change with age.
The old wall is yet my best friend in my
       mind's imagery.
Who says that walls are barriers to friendships?

THOUGHT: I recall the first black and white TV my parents purchased; it was a wonderful invention. The times were simple, as
well as the programming!

BLACK AND WHITE TV

The old black and white TV was the best;
It stood stoically in the corner of the room at rest.
Howdy Doody was my babysitter who watched me
        day after day;
In the evenings we watched shows as a family
        and laughed and laughed.
We surfed the two channels available on TV.
As a group, we watched Ed Sullivan, Gracie Allen,
        and Jackie Gleason.
The revolutionary TV brought us so much fun!
Things were simpler back in the 1950s than today
        in 2010.
The quality of life was more relaxing, and people
        helped their neighbors without thinking about
            if they should or not.
The test patterns on the old tube help us adjust
        our sight to the hues on the TV.
Perhaps we need test patterns today
        so we can see clearly what is right;
Not the 300 channels that are on TV, but life.

THOUGHT: Do you recall the "fun fairs" your school had to raise money? They were lots of fun for friends and family!

SCHOOL FUN FAIRS

The old fun fairs held a carnival-like atmosphere.
The exhibitions consisted of cake walks, fortune telling,
    the fishing booth and dance contest too!
Our parents and teachers worked as a team to raise
    money for school materials.
Learning was fun, and *Dick and Jane*
    were our favorite books.
My fortune teller said I would become
    a millionaire; she was correct.
I am alive and healthy at sixty-two!

THOUGHT: I recall those rides on my dad's shoulders; they were the best. I got a different perspective of what the world looked like.

MY DAD'S SHOULDERS WERE MOUNTAINS

The mountain I am climbing is an astonishing hill.
My youthful arms extend out trying to touch the
     puffy blue skies that appear close to my head.
The snowy hair on the mountain top is thick and grey,
     the curls are like soft feathers to my youthful skin.
As the mountain moves down the sidewalk, twisting
     and turning, I sense love and belonging.
I spring back and forth on the mountain's top;
I bounce upon the rugged boulders like a man
     riding a horse.
The tons of rocks I sit upon are unlike
     any I have felt in my young life.
The strong and striking boulders are my daddy's shoulders.
The strong stones are the foundation of my life.
On top of the peak I find love and freedom.
My dad always made sure that I would never fall from
     his high mountain!
It was wonderful to get a different point of view about life
     while I was riding on cloud nine!
Life took on different tints and connotations on the
     special day that I rode high in the sky.
All quests come to an end; this day would be no different.
As I slip off the boulders and slide down the valleys,
     I bounced onto the sidewalk....
"Life here, I view from a different perspective."
"It just is."

THOUGHT: The mansion was big, yet little!

THE BIG BUT LITTLE MANSION

When I was the ripe old age of ten, my grandpa's abode
was a life-size mansion!
I was in awe of the immense living room, bedroom, and
kitchen.
As I grew older, the rooms appeared to be shrinking,
or perhaps was I getting taller?
At the age of sixteen, I would stoop below the doorways
so I would not bump my head.
These now tiny rooms held so many cousins, uncles, aunts,
and friends.
At age sixty-two I have a gigantic grin on my face.
I drove back to Freeport to the home where I spent
countless hours and days.
As I approached the house, it appeared so diminutive.
The mansion, which was built back in the 1930s, is a shanty
compared to the houses we live in today.
I speculate it was not the size of the tiny house that made
me feel it was so large, but it was my grandparents
cousins', mom's, dad's, sister's, and aunts' love.
Flashing back, I eavesdrop into the parties to hear
laughter, see love, and all my relatives.
I ascertain a sense of oneness I have not experienced
in many years.
I taste and smell the aroma of Grandma's homemade cookies.
The small rooms are big again in my mind because of love.
I suddenly come back to reality and see
how it really appears; small and worn out.
It is not the physical structure of a home, but the contents
which live within the frame of a domicile that personifies
life!
I would say there is nothing better than a child's viewpoint.

THOUGHT: "It's Howdy Doody time!

HOWDY DOODY

"Its Howdy Doody time,"
     and the show was so refined.
I once knew a puppet and he was not a Muppet.
His name was Howdy Doody and he was a cutie.
He had forty-eight freckles on his face and
     his smile was big as the Rio Grande.
Yeah man, this dude was quite a dandy.
Ask Buffalo Bob, he will tell you,
     that Howdy was a mellow fellow.

THOUGHT: Remember Phineas T. Bluster?

PHINEAS T. BLUSTER

Do you recall Phineas T. Bluster?
He was Doodyville's creative major.
Whenever he was surprised, you
        could tell it in his eyes.
He lifted his eyebrows; he and Howdy were not pals.
Delly Dolly was the major's confidant and friend...
So the story goes -- the mayor and Delly stepped on
        Howdy's toes.
Flub-a-dub we really liked; he was eight animals in one
        and quite a sight!

THOUGHT: Do you recall Clarabell and Doodyville?

CLARABELL

Clarabell lived in Doodyville; he was a colorful clown;
His baggy white zebra costume made him look profound.
This silly clown carried a tiny chest, just beneath
      his clown-like vest.
In his box he placed a horn to answer yes or no
      when asked a question on the show.
A bottle of seltzer was his weapon of choice, since
      he could not shoot back with his voice!
He sprayed Uncle Bob in the face, when he got
      out of place.
Yet Uncle Bob loved Clarabell and his clown-like face!

THOUGHT: Those long summer days and nights never seem to end;
they were filled with laughter, fun, and joy.

THOSE LONG SUMMER DAYS AND NIGHTS

The lazy and hazy days of summer were in the
      1950s and 1960s.
Children fooled around playing house, marbles,
      jumping rope, and hop-scotch.
The boys congregated with their cowboy-like
      outfits, such as Roy Rogers.
The girls took their mother's clothesline ropes
      and jumped up and down.
We guys would draw a circle in the dirt and call friends
      over to shoot marbles.
The girls could be heard calling out numbers as they jumped
      and skipped around.
On the sidewalk you saw chalk squares with numbers
      inside.
The name of the game was hop-scotch; hip-hop-hip-hop…
Don't touch outside the box!
Those mellow flowing summer days appeared to never end.
After playing and pretending, we could hear our
      Mothers' distinctive voices calling us to come to dinner.
Dropping our treasure of toys, we would zoom
      to the supper tables.
With our dirty hands, faces, scuffed knees, and torn
      jeans, we plopped down on the chairs.
We looked like there had been a major wind storm
      and we got in the middle of the gale!
The steamy hot dogs tasted like a premium steak;
The mustard, relish, and onions added to our palate.
Gulping down our food, we zoomed out the doors
      to play in the evening's breezes.
We guys would grab broom handles that we used for bats.
We played whiffle ball until darkness,

Our yards were Wrigley Field and Comiskey Park in Chicago.
The girls invited their friends to come inside and play with
      paper dolls.
As the sun was going down in the west, so was our day
      and evening that was filled with joy.
Before retreating to bed, we would all gather on the porch
      and make plans for the next day.
We did not like to hear our parents' final call,
"It is bed time."
Yet sleeping and dreaming as a kid were not all that bad either!

THOUGHT: As a Vietnam veteran I will never forget my brothers and sisters who took the fall...they did not get back to "The World."

COLLEGE AND NAM

In the revolutionary sixties,
College was a place for the rich hippies.
Students despised the Vietnam War;
Lives were being slaughtered by the score.
The military draft was unfair; the poor fought for the rich
        and perished in despair.
The war made no sense; yet it came at such an expense.
Revolution wore her face on a nation that wanted change;
The ruthless war brought disaster and pain.
This battle was like none other; it divided moms, dads,
        sisters and brothers.
We were young and bright, yet stupid in history's sight.
Our views were varied and change took a different pace.
Vets came back to the world wanting respect;
All we got was spit in the face.
Only God knows why this war was necessary.
I give my applause to all Nam's vets who repose
        in Arlington Cemetery.
Your heroic names are embedded on The Wall;
At Heaven's Gate you will wait for us all.

THOUGHT: Generations come and go, yet war still is our major foe. We all yearn for peace, but she appears to be elusive.

THE PEACE SIGN

The shape V is still flashing today in its unique way.
The worldwide symbol entails peace in all
    the nations.
Go to China, Japan, and Russia too;
You can observe signs of peace, however few.
Many decades have come and gone;
Yet we sing war's painful songs.
Why does fighting weigh on nations' minds?
I know not why, can't they interpret the peace sign?
V

THOUGHT: "Does only God know why?

COLLEGE CAMPUSES AND VIETNAM

In the sixties, college students debated the Nam War.
The government's draft was knocking on our front doors;
Southeast Asia, citizens did not want to explore.
Many of the rich kids got a break; they went to college
        before it was too late.
Poor blacks and whites took on the nation's plight;
To me this was not right.
Fighting for justice in another nation was such a disgrace;
We could not define equality in America, our home place.

THOUGHT: You tell me!

THE SWORDS OF DEATH

The Wailing Wall at Arlington felt many hands
      touch her face.
Tears of sorrow cleansed the heroes' names
      that appear in no other place.
Embedded deeply into marble are men and women
      that would not live tomorrow.
The Nam vets who fought for freedom were called from
      us to their hollow cold graves with sorrow.
Heroes of World War II they were not at all;
Go ahead and ask our citizens what they thought of their call.
I say, "Come you 'citizens' of the sixties and notice
      your compatriots who took the fall."
Their names are frozen on the stoic wall.

THOUGHT: What is your definition of war?

FREEDOM'S FACE IS A GRAVE

The tears of red drip down freedom's face;
Let's all sing songs of sorrow with grace.
The American flag is adorned with blood and plight;
This Revolutionary War flag never forgot the faces
     who fought wars wrong or "right."
Freedom was battled for in an unjust Vietnam War;
The graves of Arlington are standing for you to explore.
It is never too late to salute our heroes' fate;
Graves have faces and families too!

THOUGHT: One generation gives to the next through revolution.

WOMEN'S LIBERATION

Women have come a long way;
Thanks to NOW who created the stage.
The feminine charisma came alive,
    and Betty Friedan was the surprise!
Her book told lots of tales of women's rights
    that were won.
Women of 2010, give thanks to a boomer
    way back when....
NOW made a difference, and now you can!

THOUGHT: Did you enjoy the stock car races on the old half mile dirt tracks? It was fun and we all had our favorite drivers to cheer as dirt clouds spewed into the stands.

HOT ROD RACES

The old half mile dirt track was the place to be on
    Sunday evenings.
People labored throughout the week in anticipation of
    going to the oval dusty track.
I was ten years young when I attended my first race;
It was fun going to the track and eating a hot dog with
    mustard and relish, and slurping a big coke.
I would scream for my favorite driver, Joe Finn, as he
    zoomed and roared around the track.
Dry dirt would fly into the air and land in my Coke;
For some reason, the dust added to the flavor
    of the Coke and to the excitement of the race.
Watching cars flip and flop and crash into
    each other was quite a rush.
I did not want anyone to get hurt if they got into a crash.
Those Sunday nights were fun, being with
    my friends and just being a kid!

THOUGHT: I recall the days when sports were fun and not just played for big money as they are today. Advanced technology in equipment, money, and big business now dominate the sports world.

BASEBALL WAS THE REAL DEAL

Back in the late fifties and sixties, baseball was
    the All-American sport.
Fans listened to WGN while doing yard work,
    cleaning the house, and sunbathing.
Banks, Santo, and Williams were household
    Cub names.
Today baseball concerns drugs, attorneys,
    and big business.
The average fan can't go the ballpark today
    without spending hundreds of dollars.
The three-dollar ticket of years gone by
    no longer exists!
Today we take front row seats on our decks
    or on the couch…eating tube steaks.
Our lounge chairs are box seats where we relax
    and imagine the setting of the ballpark
        in our creative minds.
I can see Harry Carey now up in the blue sky;
"Let me hear ya now, a one and a two and a
    what has happened to the game!"
"Hand me a cold Bud!"

THOUGHT: Major social and economic events influence the person we are molded into in life.

CREW CUTS AND MORE

We fellows had "at attention" crew cuts;
We wore mellow checkered shirts and jeans.
Our beards and long hair gave others
the impression that we were radicals; which we were!
Our turtleneck shirts strangled us, and our
polyester pants made us itch.
The ties that adorned our necks were sleek
and slim, like the Beatles wore.
We enjoyed our culture of dress, music, and art;
when Kennedy and King died so suddenly,
so did our colorful minds and ways of life.

THOUGHT: The songs of the sixties were poetic and made a romantic statement; rock and roll made us twist and shout.

GIVE ME SOME OLD TIME MUSIC

Moon River, wider than a mile,
Where the Boys Are someone waits for me...
Will You Love Me Tomorrow, even though tonight I am
    yours?
Blue Moon, you saw me standing alone...
The Lion Sleeps Tonight...in the jungle,
    the mighty jungle.
These songs' lyrics struck my heart and soul!
What has gone wrong with the songs of 2010?
We old boomers want to twist and dance again!

THOUGHT: I would like to ask the boomers, "Where were you when John F. Kennedy was shot?"

JOHN F. KENNEDY'S DEATH

On November 22, 1963 I was living life, feeling free.
I remember standing in the corridor after PE waiting to
      pass to the next class, to take an American History test.
Around the corner, without warning, came our PE teacher,
      Mr. Smith, with a face appearing forlorn.
He screamed the president was shot and hit in the head
      with a bullet; we stood still in silence from that moment.
John F. Kennedy, the 35th president of the United States
      died while in a Dallas hospital.
We students stood stock-still and had sullen
      expressions on our faces.
"Who would desire to harm a president that was doing a
      colossal job domestically and internationally?"
Questions about the murder zoomed through our minds;
We all sought after reasons "why?"
After school on that bleak and barren day,
      we all assembled; we cried, hugged and prayed.
From the east coast to the west coast and around the world,
      people were in distress;
Our everyday activities came to a quieting rest.
I halfheartedly ate and slept for several days;
The day, November 22, 1963, is eternally brailled
      in my mind and soul; I continued to pray.
The traits of PTSD for millions of people
      are alive today from the assassination.
The countenance of America and the world was altered
      forever; our sense of direction needed
            examination!

THOUGHT: The mini skirt made many heads turn; it was a revolution in the clothing industry and many people enjoyed the invention.

MINISKIRTS

Ah, that miniskirt is diminutive and fun;
The garment stood above the knees
    and us guys it pleased.
The kilt started her cruise across the sea;
England is where she was born.
Enterprising female youth dressed for style
    and many tried to scorn…
To this day, I give the miniskirt a high five;
You brought my eyes alive…
Wow!

THOUGHT: How can you describe your attitude while growing up in the 1960s?

A DECADE TO LIVE FOR

The 1960s was a decade to define;
We were all characters of many kinds!
Immature behaviors were running around
    the radical nation; youth sought after a solid
        foundation.
We yearned to generate a better human race;
Our priorities were civil rights and to stop a war
    of disgrace and plight.
We, radicals, made our statements plain and loud;
As Paul Kantner of the group "Jefferson Airplane,"
    stated, "If you cannot remember anything
        about the sixties, you weren't there."

THOUGHT: Do ya recall those round things that spin around and around! We could put them around our waist, neck, and feet!

HULA HOOP

The hula hoop was red, green, blue, and yellow.
We would take her and have contests with other fellows.
Twist, turn, turn, twist, and spinning fast too;
At the end of the day my hips were sore; how about you?

THOUGHT: The electric football game provided hours and hours of fun during the holidays and in the summer.

ELECTRIC FOOTBALL

I remember the football games I played indoors
      upon the dining room table.
I was the coach, player, and fan along with my friends.
The green tin field was the plain that the players
      ran and played on.
As a quarterback I positioned the players and arranged
      their every play.
I enjoyed calling the pass where I would flick a little
      piece of cotton from the quarterback's arm.
Those cold wintry days, we played for hours and hours.
Today the electric football game is a fable,
      the frame rests on a museum's table.

THOUGHT: Mr. Potato Head was used for more than a toy; he was symbolic socially and politically.

DO YOU KNOW THE
GREATNESS OF "THE HEAD"?

In 1987 Mr. Potato Head was a high-class citizen.
He spoke for the American Cancer Society
    in a smoky nation.
Mr. P spoke on part of the "Great American Smoke Out,"
His personality saved many lives, without a doubt.
The year 1992, Mr. Potato Head stood for fitness and fame
His photos stood on posters and billboards trying to
    help a flabby nation.
The League of Women Voters asked Mr. P to be on their
    team; this helped his self-esteem.
His message encouraged women to get out and vote
    and to speak their minds.
I ask you, "If a potato can do all of this for our country,
    what can you do for the potato?"
I think I will never eat a potato again!
Mr. Potato Head is forever my friend!

THOUGHT: Mr. Potato Head was fun to play; it was keeping track of all his parts that caused me trouble!

MR. POTATO HEAD

Mr. Potato Head was born in the year 1952.
Yup, he possessed two eyes, feet, hands, and two mouths!
His four noses helped him smell different scents.
For an Idaho Potato, he was entertaining to play with.
His brother was Spud; his sister was called Sister Yam.
The spud family is included in the Toy Hall of Fame.
To this day I do not like fried, baked, or mashed potatoes.
The potato family is quite an historic fable;
But not cooked for my dining room table!

THOUGHT: John Kennedy is one of my favorite presidents.

ASK WHAT YOU CAN DO FOR YOUR COUNTRY

John Kennedy declared many years ago,
"Ask not what your country can do for you,
      but what can you do for your country."
This famous quotation is deep within my breast;
I glimpse back to see if Americans have put
      this quote to test.
Our mighty nation has waxed and waned;
We have gone through toil and pain.
The Nam War many died for reasons not so grand.
Now Iraq, Afghanistan, and Iran; we must take a stand.
Wars appear to be a never-ending game;
Technology has come far; scientists, doctors, teachers,
      and preachers are forging new ways to life.
I yet want to ask, "What have you done for your country
      today, have you passed Kennedy's test?"
Violence, poverty, crime, natural disasters, and more…
      are rapping at our front doors…
No matter whom we yearn to point the finger at and blame;
We are all a part of life's endless games.
I yell out to all my sisters and brothers,
"We have a nation like none other;
Get out and volunteer your expert skills;
Stop taking drugs for thrills."
We Americans must never quit,
Let's keep our health and have grit.
Exercise your mind and body and stay fit.
Again, "Ask what you can do for your country,
      not what your country can do for you."

Thought: Whatever positive or negative knowledge and feelings we give away will be passed on to other generations; words and actions are powerful and can break or make a family, church, or nation.

BOOMERS ARE ONE OF MANY

Baby boomers are countless in a world approaching
    seven billion inhabitants.
We cross over two generations and have impacted social,
    political, and economic changes.
Each boomer, although from a set of two different decades,
    has made the world a better place through their
        counter-revolutionary actions!
As a collection, we have shown compassion, taken action,
    and knocked down some of the fences
        of racism and sexism.
Acting in love, compassion, empathy, and some radical
    viewpoints, we queried a government's philosophy
        about war and international relations.
Today we must recognize the new generations and
    their unique viewpoints…
There are more viewpoints than ours in the world
    to listen to and understand.
This is genuine love!
No fences, walls, or concrete structures can beat "all"
    of our positive contributions to the political and social
        revolution taken place today.
Fences, walls, or any structures do not make good neighbors --
Ask Robert Frost!

THOUGHT: Recall that sticky pink Bazooka bubble gum? We enjoyed the sugary taste and the dentists loved the gum even better -- it brought them business!

I AM FOREVER BLOWING BAZOOKA

In the candy land of my youthful dreams;
I savor penny candy of red, black, and green.
The pink I adored the best; it is Bazooka and the gum
    made me laugh.
No, don't be silly and assume the bubble gum made me high,
    it was the comics that wrapped the sticky stuff
        that made me giggle and sigh.
I rip open the wrapper and pop the pink
    precious gum in my drooling mouth.
With twisting and turning tongue, I blow bubbles
    until my tongue goes south!
The bubbles I blow are not gigantic enough;
I pop another portion into my bulging mouth and go puff, puff;
Fighting for breath, I blow and blow until the biggest
    bubble is the best...pop it goes all over my face.
My appearance turns a funny pink!
I won the contest between my friends and now I grin;
You think I would be forever blowing bubbles in the air;
No, I am just a bubblehead blowing gum!

THOUGHT: Those beautiful Schwinn bikes were awesome to ride; I put a mirror on the handlebars, streamers on the handles, and placed balloons on the spokes to make the engine roar.

SHINY SCHWINN

My shiny Schwinn bike was the best;
It was silver and red, it passed my test.
Multi-colored steamers surged from the handlebars
     as I zoomed along the streets.
A silver headlight was mounted on the front bars;
At night I rode my ride with my light as my guide.
I tied balloons on my spokes; my bike sounded
     like a car, this is no joke.
Flap, flap, flap was my engine's roar;
Pop, pop, and pop, my engine was no more,
However my ride still got me to the store!

THOUGHT: Can you recall those fun times you enjoyed playing with old friends? I learned a lot about friendship from my neighborhood friends and playmates. I enjoyed playing basketball from dawn to dusk in the old hood.

BASKETBALL IN THE STREET

We didn't have a lot of places where we could engage
      in recreational basketball; the kids in my hood
          could not afford to belong to the YMCA.
Our much loved basketball court stood majestically on Miami
      Street in Freeport, Illinois.
My friends, the Milligan boys, prepared a basketball court for
      the kids on the block.
We guys would spend hours in rain, snow, sleet, and hail
      shooting hoops.
The games of twenty-one, risk it, and one on one were
      played all day and night long;
I would be remiss if I did not mention HORSE!
The children, including myself, came from lower
      middle class families who lived in the neighborhood.
We were poor money-wise; but rich in friendships.
Many of us who played hoops went on and made something
      of ourselves.
The Mulligan boys and I turned out to be teachers.
Al, one of my friends, turned out to be an attorney,
      and others went into business.
I am proud to say that we rose above the gangs, hardships,
      and obstacles we faced.
Poverty can make a statement -- however, so can genuine
      friendships and an old basketball hoop!

THOUGHT: Revolution comes at an expense!

GROOVY MAN

Groovy man, groovy man is heard from the crowd.
Peace signs are flashing and people talking loud.
An opposing revolution is happening, but at what cost?
The government of the USA did not listen to what we
        boomers had to say… they were the boss.
Many sought after women's rights and their voices
        to be heard;
Racism was flourishing, which was absurd.
Dr. Martin Luther King was an organizer born on the run;
He was trying to seek equality with his God-like songs.
King walked many miles and sat at courthouse doors;
Human rights were his aim that many racists deplored.
First it was Kennedy and then Martin's fate;
Let us not overlook Bobby after his California debate.
He was shot to death and added to the Kennedy family's fate.
Man went to the moon to explore one more place;
Why could he not stay on Earth to manage the human race?
Groovy man, groovy man was part of our times;
These are fine words; perhaps rather sublime.
Not cool, I would have to say…let's stay at our
        own front doors and away from outer space.

THOUGHT: Has there ever been peace in the world?

THE DOVE

The symbol of the dove flies over every part of the Earth
      showing her emblem to those lovers of peace.
You can observe the bird pasted on billboards, on necklaces,
      and her wings spread widely on shirts.
Today, the dove of peace is perched in my soul,
      as well as others' hearts.
In the 1960s, the bird labored so hard to bring
      calm to a country in mayhem.
Things have not changed as far as war since the 1960s.
      Disputes are currently being fought, and the dove
      yearns to embrace one thing: peace.

THOUGHT: Do you remember the recreation nights you had at the local YMCA or YWCA?

REC NIGHT

On Fridays we would have recreation night;
We slurped pop and twisted and shouted.
We dudes would put butch wax on our crews
       to make our hair go straight up!
The girls would wear scarves around their
       necks, and penny loafers.
Dancing to the old 45 rpm records was great.
The DJ would announce a song that we could
       line dance to…
I tripped over my feet and felt like a big duck out of water.
Trying to look cool for the gals was a hard thing to do at times!
Dancing, laughing, and kidding around was fun.
"Hey, do ya wanna dance under the moonlight?"
PS: "However, no line dancing!"

THOUGHT: Christmas back in the 1950s was fun and exciting; there were many fun activities that I did with my family and individually. I entered the annual Christmas coloring contest sponsored by the local newspaper; it was fun and I would look forward to it every year.

THE CHRISTMAS COLORING CONTEST

The local merchants sponsored an annual
    coloring contest during the Christmas season.
The newspaper, *The Journal Standard,* placed
    various holiday photos to cut out and color in
        the paper.
I would retrieve some crayons and shade the various
    photos to send to the businesses.
Around December 1st of each year, I would search like
    a detective in the paper to seek the pages that
        I could cut out and color.
The age of five was the first time I started to explore
    my artistic talents by coloring in the pictures.
I recall getting irritated because I could not stay
    within the lines of the figures.
Despite my lack of eye and hand coordination,
I sent my labor of genius to
    the merchants to be judged.
Year after year, I mailed copies to the retailers;
I was never selected!
The last year I would enter the competition was age twelve.
Guess what? I got second place!
Five years of toil got me second place;
The owners of the local businesses probably
    felt sorry for me!
To this day I wonder how the judges could grade fairly
    all the pieces that were sent in; their rubric
        must have been strict!
Nonetheless, this activity was exciting for me and

I continued to toil until age twelve.
Today, as a senior citizen, I am not a Van Gogh,
  however, I enjoy cutting photos
   out of the paper to this day!
I would do much better staying within the lines;
However, my color choices for the pictures
  might be wild; my eyes aren't what they used to be!

THOUGHT: I recall with fondness what my mother, sister, and I did at Christmas the first time at age five.

THAT FIRST CHRISTMAS

When do you recall your first Christmas?
I was five or six years when Santa first brought
    me gifts down the chimney!
Mom and Dad did not have lots to give materially,
But they made Christmas time memorable.
The first Christmas I received a train set
    and a Roy Rogers outfit!
The train was an electric one; on Christmas
        morning, I got up and saw the train
            tracks circling around the Christmas tree.
The locomotive was one that you could put a little pill into
        and add water; steam would flow out the top!
The cowboy outfit was fun and I thought I was one tough dude
        with my holster and guns on!
Before Christmas, we went out as a family and acquired
        a prized tree!
Dad drove to the local dairy house where a special lot
        of trees waited for our arrival.
Every year we purchased a Charlie Brown tree;
They were the best, we adorned them with
        glittering adornnments, making the tree
            appear beautiful.
Dad brought an old clothesline to tie the tree
        to the top of the car.
As a group we sang traditional Christmas songs
        to the dairy house and back.
Arriving home, we allowed the tree to sit overnight
        so her limbs could expand.
The next day, we would adorn the tree with
        ornaments.
Mom popped popcorn and we strung the kernels

with needles; Mom got angry if I ate too
much popcorn -- she would have to make more!
It was forever putting those tiny kernels of corn on the string!
Next, we would get colored construction paper and cut
out strips that we made into circles.
The red and green strings of circles would go around the tree.
To this day, I remember that rubber applicator and hard glue
we used to paste the pieces together.
First, we would place the old fashioned Christmas lights
on Charlie Brown, next the strings of popcorn
and finally the colored paper.
After the tree was decorated, we sipped hot chocolate
and sang Christmas carols.
Simplicity, joy, simplicity, joy, simplicity;
Our family Christmas was the best!

THOUGHT: What special toys were in your treasure chest when you were a small lad in the 1950s?

LINCOLN LOGS

I went shopping today on December 2009 for Christmas gifts.
There were countless novel toys on display; I was
    on "instant overload" as a shopper.
One plaything caught my eye as I meandered down the fully
    stocked aisle.
Lincoln Logs were one of my favorite toys as a child;
They make the logs still today!
I flashback and see myself digging into my
    old toy chest, gathering the scattered logs.
I am building a log cabin; I pick a place in the yard
    where I can have trees and construct a river around a new
        building.
The Lincoln Logs sparked my creativity and helped
    me through some long play days!
"Excuse me sir, may I help you with something?"
I suddenly awaken back to reality.
"Yes miss," I say.
"I would like a set of Lincoln Logs."
"Great," she replies.
"I bet they are for one special child?"
"Yes, they are for me!"

THOUGHT: As a small child, I had the opportunity to wear those sexy yellow raincoats and Daffy Duck hoods!

RAINCOATS AND WINTER BOOTS

On rainy days I had to wear my mustard colored raincoat.
The big rubber hat I put on my head made me feel
    like a gigantic wild duck.
To add insult to injury, those stupid tin buckles on the boots
    froze when the temperature got too cold!
In the winter when it snowed, the buckles froze over
    and I had to tug and tug to get my boots off!
Sure, I was successful, my socks and shoes all came out
    at once -- my pink ice-covered toes were happy, though!

THOUGHT: When did you first read *Dick and Jane*?

A GOOD READ

"Oh, let us have fun," said Dick to Jane,
"You carry Tim, the teddy bear,
    and we will play a game."
"Oh see Spot run, oh see Spot run…"
Today this book should be on *New York's*
    Bestseller List!

THOUGHT: Before I go on to my love and nature poems, I would like to end with an all-inclusive thought about the era of the 1950s and 1960s.

BOOM ZAP PLOP

Boom, bam, zap; we initiated a counter revolution.
Zap, bam, boom; a Vietnam War was going strong.
Boom, bam, zap; major protest occurred
      all over the nation.
Boom, bam, zap; two Kennedys, and Martin Luther
      King were gone.
Zap, bam, boom; we yearned to have life our way!
Zap, bam, boom; we made a difference…
Boom, bam, zap; the years went by…
Today we glance back and sigh.
"What ifs" and how could our decades have been different?
We were a cohort, one of a kind; our history
      will forever be a mystery.
Boom, bam, zap; we made a difference.

CHAPTER FIVE

BABY BOOMER'S POEMS:
LIFE AND NATURE

In this section, I will share "life" and nature poetry with you that I have written over many years. We are all poets and can write our own life stories though the various verses we compose. As Robert Frost once stated, "A good poem begins in delight and ends in wisdom." By reading my works, I hope you can take and apply some concepts that may enrich your life's journey.

SEIZE THE DAY

Seize the day, don't cast it away,
Impeccable is life even though there is strife.
The elements of life are many
       and they don't cost one penny!
The stars radiate at night and the birds
       take graceful flight.
The sun warms the earth and daily there is birth;
The oceans are vast and blue, for all of nature to view.
Life is special, you see; electrifying and free.
Seize the day, again I can say, and capture life in your own way.

YOUR DREAMS

Keep in touch with your dreams, for they are yours alone.
They are glittering stars within your mind and soul.
Put wings on your dreams and soar to new heights.
For in life's clouds your dreams will appear;
Cup your hands and do not fear, those glittering
Stars will brightly appear,
Only if you believe in your dreams!

MOMENTS IN TIME

Do you ever feel that someone is on your shoulder
      when in moments of doubt?
Suddenly there are whispering winds of faith
      blowing into your soul and with
            something to say to you.
Feeling blue, rivers of tears flow down
      your face into a well of emptiness;
Unexpectedly the Day Star comes out and warms your soul.
Those old sinister clouds move east and new golden
      rays of hope appear.
Hold on to your mindset; angels like to sit on high places!

A GOLDEN PINK RIBBON

Pink flowers that grow;
Pink birds that fly and flow;
Pink is seen in Heaven's skies.
Pink provides beauty in the rainbow's arch up high.
Pink Easter eggs decorate the Sunday table.
Pink Easter Bunny's ears stand tall and stable.
Pink slippers are worn upon women's feet.
Pink rings grip ladies' hands, bright and sleek.
Pink lemonade quenches ladies' thirst;
A crimson Cadillac was Elvis' first.
Minuscule pink fingers are on a girl's hand;
Cherry dimples on their faces that grow and expand.
The tint of pink is a bestowing grace;
Pink silky ribbons in women's hair
     show dignifying grace and flare.
The best is a pink ribbon that we pin
     on our chest;
The symbol pink will beat cancer;
If given a chance…
Awareness!

SLUMBERING AWAKE IN THE WOODS

I am lying in the dark and damp forest at night;
Positioning my weary body and head on the ground
      I peer at the luminaries in the sky.
Canis Major woofs and wags her star-studded tail in delight.
The Big Dipper is quenching my thirst with water like ale;
Lamenting wolves' echoes I hear in a far distance.
The wise Owl hoots and screeches in the night while
      watching stoically with her two headlights.
Whispering and cooling winds propel the brown hairs
      on top of my head.
The silence of the night is quiet, yet loud to my restless mind.
I take notice of the gurgling creek as she meanders down
      the lazy terrain of the forest's bed.
Hey, I think Henry David Thoreau would say that
      reposing in the forest is the way to go!
That is, slumbering awake in the woods is not that bad,
Only if I could sleep…yawn, yawn, and snore.

THE DAY STAR

The Day Star blazes with intense love and radiation;
She tosses slanting rays from the skies like
    a high intensity beam.
The radiant rays lend a hand to compose nature's green,
      I suspect...
I feel sad for the man in the moon,
He only reflects the sun's light!
I would say he is a second class citizen compared
    to the Day Star!

MY SENSES ARE LIKE THE SANDS OF TIME

I detect with ocean rumbling to the terra firma,
     with the power of a puma.
I am inhaling the salt from the sea;
It gives me a feeling of serenity.
I feel the sands of time oozing through my toes;
It's a great sensation, don't you suppose?
I touch with care the tiny grains of sand;
I lose my spirit in nature as my mind expands.
I savor the life of the wanton sea;
I hunger for life and to be with thee.
All my sensations are varied and sublime;
They cannot be lost in the sands of time.
As my hourglass fades into the naked night,
Oh, my darling, without you life is not right.
Our love once was vast like the open sea;
Oh, my darling, why did you leave me?
Oh, my darling, why am I not yet free?

FEELING NATURE IS LIKE HEAVEN

The flaxen country grass stoops humbly to the winds.
The pompous birds rest on the protracting phone wires
      listening to all of the gossip of our greedy generation.
The flourishing fertile fields of spring are soon to
      emerge with plants to invigorate my life.
Riding like the wind on my bike I gaze and glimpse
      at nature with a feeling of awe.
The beautiful floral arrangements nature gratuitously
      shares paint a mural in my heart.
Many people painstakingly peer for God in so many
      places…
I look and find God while He brushes my heart
      with his majestically ordained paintbrush,
In a field of glory in the early spring fields of passion's fire!

THE SOUNDS OF SPRING

chirp, chirp, chirp
raindrops, raindrops, raindrops
sun shining, sun warming, sun gleaming
life is reborn

THE ASPEN TREES ARE BARREN AS HUMANS

Where has the Aspen tree gone?
Her branches that once painted
      the mountains have died and are no
         longer strong.
Why have the Aspen's foliage
      sung their last song?
Many declare that man is to blame;
Oh, what a shame!
Ecologists say it's the humans' ballgame.
Life is living with clean air, not to vandalize
      the Earth without care.
People cry that caterpillars and droughts
      are to blame.
Let us stop these silly thinking games.
There are 5650 square miles of trees --
      those no longer provide a breeze.
Oh humanity, please stop and consider the tragedy.
The lush leafy tree branches no longer
      bounce and wave in the wind.
Only barren sticks abrade the clouded skies,
      this is a mortal sin!
Oh, vacant Aspens, I shed tears from my
      blue eyes.
The tree shoots no longer bring into being the
      newborn leaves…
For this I have humans to scorn.
The droughts and insects we could blame;
      however, we humans compose the game…destruction.

HAIRY WOODPECKER

Hairy Woodpecker, you have an outsized bill;
I peer at my feeder and you give me a thrill.
Your natural white back is pure as the snow;
Oh, Hairy Woodpecker, you eat and then go.
You fly away with the peanut in your mouth;
Away you zoom to your home, no doubt…
Red marks the crown on top of your head.
Fine-looking bird, where lies your bed?
You call to your friends with a unique sound.
Peek, peek, and peek, your reverberations resound.
Oh, bird of color and grace; you have a home
      in my heart; you are a bird so profound.

VISIONS

Do not pursue another's dreams;
The secrets of your thoughts are
     twine that binds your soul.
The wings of your spirit provide
     you with pathways to go.
Your unique ideas are treasures only to you;
Again I say, see your pathways, and to your
     own heart be true.

SNOWBIRDS ARE GOLDEN

The Juncos in December flutter
    to the top of the bird feeder
        in quest of a carte du jour.
            for sunflower seeds.
Their blustery white breasts shine against
    the fluffy fallen snow.
The chubby birds do their bobbling
    strides and twist their heads
        as if they are performing
            "the snowbirds' boogie."
Their light smack of talk suggest they
    are enjoying their snack!
Perhaps I will join them someday
    for a crunchy lunch.
They eat French cuisine;
I will bring the wine.

THE BIRDS OF PASSAGE

The flora and fauna are akin to the moon;
They wax and wane with the seasons to bloom.
The blackberries are a yummy treat;
The white flowers are awesome to see.
The birds too love the sight; they enjoy feasting
      while they are in flight.
Tasting, the Pladus dines next to none;
They consume their meals while they are on the run.
Food sustains these birds on their flights;
The birds of passage work day and night.
Thanks to the Prunua Pladus, this is part of nature's delight!

THE EARLY MORNING SQUAWK

In the early morning hours I hear a squawk outside my
      window; it is a raspy "jay jay" calling me to sing.
The ratchet-like beckoning brings my heart to life,
The hues of blue, gray, and black are reflected sunlight.
This beautiful bird of nature creates quite a scene,
      beneath my feeder the Blue Jay continues
          to scream.
Ah, I imagine he is my alarm clock so early this morn,
      but then again, it sounds like I am being scorned!
Perchance I forgot to sprinkle food for him to eat
      on the platform beneath the evergreen tree?
I gaze distantly at the stand which rests quaintly
      above the ice-covered ground; sure enough,
          then no food is to be found!
I spring into action and run into the garage;
I scamper to gather nuts, sunflowers,
      cracked corn, and more.
Who says this Jay is not yelling at my door?
The rogue-sounding Jay has me flying like
      a bird; don't you think that is absurd?
Sometimes I imagine she is screaming like a hawk;
However, when she is hungry she plainly talks.
"Feed me, please!"

TEARS ARE JOY

The raindrops descend as tears upon the roses;
Flowing lightly down the stem
     and back into the Earth's well-to-do soil.
Sorrow is growth when we do not recognize it.

LISA, THE BIRD WATCHER

Lisa observes through her lenses
    as an Owl would at night searching for prey.
She eavesdrops for sounds of diverse birds.
Lisa differentiates the Latin names of all her friends;
    the catalog goes on in her mind from beginning to end.
I love this bird observer -- you would too,
    she feels affection for birds and respects their habitats.
The bird watcher focuses her camera like eyes
    on prized trophies such as the Red-tailed Hawk;
        Pileated Woodpecker and the Snowy Owl.
Banding birds has been her passion
    for more than two decades.
Every Saturday morning she awakens
    and leaves for the banding station.
The stories she tells about birds seem
    legendary; she tells them across the nation.
This naturalist to me flies high with Cupid!

OUR LOVE IS OWLISH

Gazing at birds through our rounded glasses,
   we are eager to categorize the
     winged ones into special classes.
Focusing the binocular, Lisa and I observe a Snowy Owl!
The extraordinary bird is out of her natural habitat;
   she is further south than she should be.
The precious bird is viewed; she is quite beautiful!
The ashen owl with a puffed up breast
   is keeping warm on the border
    of a barren cornfield.
I question how she took the long flight south,
   ending up miles from her assigned bed?
Is it because of the global warming, or did
   she have to fly far to get her prey?
Lisa and I share love in many ways through
   viewing God's natural creation as a team.
Today, the sight of the Snowy Owl is precious and one
   "of those moments in time."
Desiring that the lost Owl will find its way back north,
   we meander toward the car, wondering what our
    next natural find will be?
I wish I could pose this question to the wise owl,
   but she is trying to figure other things out
    in the cold corn field!
Perhaps she is "lost in time," just like her viewers!

THE WISTFUL WINDS

Sauntering the barren paths of the northern
    Wisconsin woods I am surveying
        for wildlife.
As the wistful winds whisper gently to my
    thirsting soul, the topography
        of the serene woods is a sight to behold.
I am surprised as an eagle glides over my head
    as she is peering for dinner on the forest's bed.
The eagle is another blessing to God's Earth,
    possessing an ample wing span and girth.
Oh, in the sheltered forests I always yearn to be,
    where my soul is calm and free.
I invite you to draw closer with me to this special
    enchanted land.
In the calm and majestic birch trees the birds
    resonate melodies.
Ah, I have passion for these quaint and quiet times.
    in God's layer of the wild forest...
I am always at my best; just the birds and me at rest.

WINDS AND EAGLES

The breezes whisper the feelings of eagles
    riding high on heaven's clouds.
Airstreams give wings to their flights as they float
    and glide proud.
Like the eagle's getaway, love rides on the winds
    of heaven's clouds.
I want to ride like an eagle and fly with
    Cupid-like wings to let my lover know that I care.
I am lonely as an eagle floating in outer space.
Winds, let me ride with your power
    and embrace the warm sun's rays.
Give me a second chance with love
    and fly as an eagle with grace.

CUNNING CARDINAL

His reflection is highlighted on the windowpane;
He slams again and again into the glass
     without rethinking.
Like someone rapping all over again at
     the front door; the Cardinal
          wants to get in and explore...
Thud, thud, thud...
Silence...thud, thud, and thud...silence.
Protecting his terrain involves vanity
     I might even say insanity!
His red and black markings make
     him our Mr. State Bird.
This handsome creature reminds me of
     some humans who constantly
          appear in mirrors
               trying to discover beauty!
I will be right back; I have to check myself out!

FEBRUARY IS MUD

The month of February is quagmire and rain;
Its murky traits lie upon the frozen Earth's terrain.
Birds and humans too search for provisions...
       sometimes in pain!
The sun has traveled south,
       not here in the north to sustain.
Keeping the earth's temperature just right,
There are times the sun gets
       downright cold and causes pain.
Brr, brr, and brr...
That February is bold!

THEY SAY IT IS ONLY A PAPER MOON

The song says that it is only a paper moon hanging
    over a cardboard sea.
I say the man in the moon is so much more
    for both you and me.
Sharing its quiet golden light within our
    hearts, we hold hands and gaze
        at her, never wanting to part.
The stars are steps to the golden moon's throne.
The stages of the moon wax and wane while
    our love goes on, listening to the lover's song.
The lyrics state it is only a canvas sky, but it is love
    as we kiss and sigh.
The universe of wonder and awe embraces
    our souls within;
The paper moon is not paper for us, it is gold;
Here is where our love starts and never ends.
Without your passion, the sky is moonless and the
    steps of stars are only hanging around.
I will rope the paper moon and scribe poems
    of love....
To let her know her light that shines enhances
    lover's love; she is not paper-thin!

NATURE IS SOOO FINE

The sweeping spring grass is green;
The golden moon glides across the sky.
The ocean's surfs kiss the land
      with water like lips;
Lapping up lovers' footprints in the sand;
Nature is sooo fine....
There is nothing better, in my mind.
Sooo fine...one of a kind...

THE MOON IS A FLASHLIGHT

The full autumn moon is glued against
    the sky.
She is a lighthouse for the Earth, her footstool.
The stars spread widely surround her beam
    as angelic gems.
The moon and her majesty make "ah" moments
    for my soul.
Shine on golden moon, shine on.
Ah and ah!

REFLECTIONS: EARLY AUTUMN

Foliage dances and sways in the early autumn
     winds like ballet dancers.
Early in the hours of the morning the frost is
     painted on the green grass.
I see the birds migrating south to find a new place
     to relax and take baths.
The earth is rotating on her axis bringing
     forth a new season soon to pass.
Fall is the time to smell the burning air and inhale
     the perfume of the smoldering leaves into
       my lungs.
Roasting marshmallows, hot dogs, and s'mores;
     in the park I like to explore.
I survey the leaves that are diverse colors;
Orange, red, and yellow are my favorite hues.
Nature is a grand artist; she takes her palette
     and paints spectacular scenes for my soul.
Her ingenuity is beyond any human's talents.
In the fall I take time to savor apple pies, eat caramels,
     bite slowly into taffy apples, and devour
       pumpkin pies.
I like fall, but then again, I just love life!

LOVE MELTS ICE

Winter is slapping and shaking my front door.
The fields of gold are spent and no longer
    around to explore.
Icicles stretch with a frigid stance;
Winter birds are landing on the feeder
    doing a line dance.
Boogie, boogie, the birds bop around;
The snowbirds retrieve seeds scattered
    on the ground.
Cardinals of red and black perch patiently
    on the evergreen trees.
Starlings pilfer peanuts like thieves in the night;
Wintry weather is the time of year that the fire burns
    just right.
The fireside is blazing with shooting flames;
Hearts are filled with nature's warmth
    as long as I am not outside!
Did I say, "winter is for the birds"?

HUMMINGBIRD

The hummer flies fluently with her buzzing-like wings;
Zooming past bushes and flowers like a jet,
    I know not why.
Her miniscule wings motor up and down;
I would say she is the friendliest bird
    in my "bird-like" town; my yard!

A FLUTE IS PASSION

Love does not take note of time;
Passion smiles and enjoys every day.
Authentic love does not enumerate
      right from wrong; it simply sings its own song.
Adoration walks hand in hand and possesses
      clear sight;
Sipping nectar of fruit and flowers it tastes
      with delight.
Love is like playing a flute with passion;
Mozart's notes float flawlessly out of a flutist's heart;
A cacophony of sounds create sparks
      igniting two lover's hearts…it takes fire!

WHAT IS A DAUGHTER?

A daughter is love and is full of joy;
She smiles, runs, and tricks employs.
Her waving pony tail sways in the winds;
A daughter just is…
I know not where to stop or begin…
Love.

FAITH IS A MIRROR OF LOVE: ADOPTION

Faith believes in things unseen...
Faith is composed of confidence, love, peace,
    joy, frustration, and perseverance.
Faith means waiting countless months to have
    a dream forged and actualized.
Faith is anxiously going on the internet to notice
    the process of your adoption taking place.
Faith means loving support from husband and wife
    during a time of challenges.
Faith means trusting people on distant continents
    whom you have never been introduced to.
Faith articulates that life is not easy;
    events will come out not the way you sought,
        but the way God's hand's wrought.
A year ago faith paid off; a pearl of love, joy,
    and wonder was given to a mom and dad.
Far away in China, a child was placed at a gate;
    for her, life was not too late.
Sophia is like a pearl.
Beautiful, well-rounded, and all people want
    to touch and embrace her beauty.
A youngster who bellows out "hi" to all strangers;
A baby who is keenly developing her own way
    in a universe approaching seven billion.
We give thanks to God for giving our family Sophia Bien.
We accept as true the people we love and nourish
    are merely mirrors of those who surround them.
Thanks, Sophia, for being our mirror of love too!

MY SECRET LOVER IS NATURE

The warm summer day emancipates
my soul with the sun's light.
The natural splendor of the sun's rays
warm my thoughts and help
capture a keen interest
in nature.
The multi-tinted Monarchs perch on the end of
waving flowers; life is reborn.
Whispering winds kiss my face with gentle
breezes...
Ah, my secret lover... nature and metamorphosis!

WE ARE RICH

As we walk along the paths of the dense forest,
      we peer at the birds balancing on the distant
            limbs of trees.
Lisa and I share the fresh fall breezes as the sun
      teases us as she shines in and out through
            the thick trees of the salient forest.
As a couple, we love God and what He has so generously
      given to us: nature.
We view the tall scented pines decorated with brown
      rugged cones...
We hear the squirrels scurrying, yet we do not see them!
We sit by the lake and eavesdrop to the loon's lonely call.
We point to the billowy clouds as they saunter at
      a snail's pace across the horizon.
We touch the butterfly's wings that flap in the
      fresh autumn air.
We scuffle through the prairie grasses as treasure
      hunters searching for gold.
We focus on the Blue Heron with her distinct identifiable features.
We both want nature to be clean and untouched.
Lisa and I are both lucky to know what wealth means;
It certainly is not on Wall Street or homes or cars supreme.
We thank God for minting our spirits and not money;
"We" are one with God...we are rich!

FAITH IS A FLAME

Faith is a golden amber friend that
      burns within our hearts until the end.
Faith is fire burning bright, lending
      hope to those without sight.
Faith is a special candle which sometimes
      flickers; she will be there when you
         always need her.
Faith just is, "she is a special keeper."
Embrace her!

DOLL HOUSES AND DAUGHTERS

Remember those days when we built doll houses,
    my daughters?
We took run of the mill cardboard waffled boxes
    and created mansions for Barbie and her friends.
Holding two tiny hands I saunter
Down the steps into the basement where we use
    our artful skills.
As a team we collect rags, paint, tin cans, and wood
    that I cut for furniture.
My house designers are Ginni and Heidi,
    my two lovely daughters; they are ages seven and nine.
Getting a huge cardboard box, I carve the dimensions for
    the big Barbie house!
Ginni and Heidi tear rags for the curtains of the abode;
They are very good interior designers.
As I take a sharp knife, the girls direct
    me where to place and cut the windows on the big box.
The rectangles soon are decorated by the colored rags
    my daughters so diligently painted and colored.
As I continue to cut, the girls say, "Daddy, be sure that
    you put a front door in, plus living rooms,
        dinning rooms, kitchens, bedrooms,
            and kitchens!"
As my architects direct me, the house begins to
    appear like a big Barbie mansion;
Both of the sisters get their watercolors out
    and paint the exterior of the house their
        favorite hues.
Next they paint the cardboard floors and walls.
Soon the residence is delightful colors of blue, pink,
    and green.
Building Barbie's house was quite a task;
After we construct the big house, we need to make furniture!

Cutting the furniture, I use soft pine for wood;
I employ a knife and small hand saw to assist me;
I cut squares and ovals for the chairs, tables, and desk.
Next, I engrave legs for the rectangles and ovals;
The girls use Elmer's glue to paste the furniture together.
With their tiny fingers, zest, and determination my
        two angels are professional furniture makers.
All there is left to be done is to invite Ken over for dinner!
My favorite ladies are now thirty-eight and forty years old!
Whenever I see them happy and smiling as women,
        my mind's camera flashes back to those memorable days.
                that only a father and his daughters can understand...
The dimples on their girl-like faces today have not changed;
Their long brown wavy hair drapes to their shoulders.
I will always see my grown and mature daughters as
        "Daddy's girls" helping me to build a mansion!
At the present, both of my daughter's homes are built
        on the foundations of their love and creativity.
However, I am glad they did not select waffled cardboard
        boxes for their walls...
But then again, maybe they would ask me to help out!

A PRONOUN PROJECT

"I" ascertained a lot from directing school social science projects
    with my daughters.
"I" learned that "I" needed a set of encyclopedias so "we"
    could do in-depth research.
"I" learned that "I" needed to have plenty of flour, newspapers,
    water, baking soda, and watercolors to aid "us" in the
        construction of the project.
"I" learned to go to the lumber yard and buy wood
    to construct the different landforms.
"I" learned to cut chicken wire for the construction of the
    inner mountain ranges;
"I" learned to cut wood out of the various wood forms
    with a jigsaw…
Oh, yes, the cans of spray paint "we" selected to use
    for the different colors of mountains, rivers, and plains
        were purchased at the hardware store by "me."
"I" had more fun than the kids working on the project!
"They" had fun putting the masterpiece together…
"I" felt proud of "them" when "they" received awards
    for a job well done.
"I" felt like "I" deserved an award too!
But what are dads for?

MY TWO CUB BEARS AND THE CUBS

We enjoyed trips to Wrigley Field's gates;
Watching the Cubs lose was part of their fate.
Eating hot dogs, sipping Coke, and more…
Our team, the Cubs, we shall forever adore!
Studying the cotton candy man trying to
      sell us his treat…but no, thanks
            it was much too sweet.
Standing and clapping when a long ball
      was hit; there was nothing better --
          the Cubs never quit.
In the seventh inning we paid attention to Harry and Ron,
      as they sang their favorite song.
"Take Me Out To the Ballgame"
      was such a big hit…
Ron and Harry never allowed their fans to quit.
We laughed and embraced shoulders as we
      swayed with the melodies of their songs…
Going to watch the Cubs we never lost: family!

CHAPTER SIX

SPECIAL NARRATIVE POEMS
AND STORIES

In chapter six, I am writing narrative poems and short stories about unique experiences that I have encountered in my life. Various poems may strike up thoughts about special life events that you have gone through in your life's journeys. I trust that some of the poems will encourage you to write and reflect on some of the unique happenings in your life.

THOUGHT: Do you recall that first youthful love? When you met that special person, you thought it would be forever!

YOUTHFUL LOVE

I see you reaching out for my love
     as you gracefully, fluently, and lovingly
          gallop through the beautiful strewn flowers.
The fresh scent of the spring air permeates our youthful
     minds and spirits,
The girlish grin on your face touches my heart
     with a rare feeling of excitement and joy.
I sense delight as I have never experienced in my
     youthful life.
Your charming grace and beauty lightens my steps
     as I plunder with anticipation
          toward you.

Yearning to embrace you and give you
     a spring-like kiss, thistles of the open field
          punch my skinny ankles,
               warning me to watch out!

The pain in my ankles tells me to watch out for
     this novel kind of love, a first love!
My throbbing heart senses a Cupid-like sting of love
     and honey.
As I come near to you, I peer through the windows
     of your soul.
An emotion of love gropes our youthful hearts with
     a big hug.
Ah, the flowers arrayed majestically in the meadow
     speak lovingly to our emotions.
They are paint brushes sweeping across our souls;
     a mural of love and devotion is painted into our minds.
The flora appears to be brighter, the air is fresher,
     and life has the golden tint of Cupid!

You are the first love I have encountered,
Cupid's passion is true, yet mystical.
"Oh, how it feels to be touched and held."
Our parents always told us, "You are too young to be in love."
How wrong they were!

In some strange way, I know this freckle-faced
        girl with waving pony tails and penny loafers
            will be mine forever!
Her girlish smile lifts me to the mountain-top of love.
I feel like I am on top of the world, looking down
        on creation; what an awesome world to behold.
Every day I comb my hair and place each
        strand tidy and neat for my new love.
I peer into the mirror countless times making sure
        my face is flower-like for you.
I write hundreds of notes and make numerous phone
        calls just to hear your voice;
In the background I hear your mother telling
        you, "Get off the phone!"

As the seasons come and go,
        so does your girlish style of hair.
Your brown wavy pony tails are no longer
        flipping and flopping in the wind.
The carefree attitude which you had no longer
        beams brightly on your face.
Our attitudes about life are changing.
"What is the adult life about anyhow?"

My voice grows deep as a bullfrog's;
Perhaps I am becoming a real man?
Little stubs of dark hair appear on
        my face like sandpaper.

We are losing our vigor
    of free and unconditional love
        that we held so precious months earlier.

The two of us are growing in different directions;
We view the world in different ways
    based on our youthful experiences.
Our "young at heart love" is starting to fade away.

After high school graduation,
    we no longer saw each other.
However, you will always be my first love.

Sixty-two years later
    as I jog by the glorious country spring fields
        puffed with flowers, I smile a boyish
            grin on my spiderwebbed face.

Wait! I see two young kids scampering
    in this spring field of flaxen flowers.
Could youthful love still be golden in 2010?
The young girl and boy are beaming with joy
    and celebrating young love.

The youths are laughing, smiling, and yelling words
    of love to each other.
I think to myself, "If only I retained that youthful
    love that all generations experience."
As I continue jogging, I begin to feel the young
    love that I possessed more than
        six decades ago in the field of dreams.
This baby boomer started running in the spring
    fields again.

The spirited, youth-like love that I once considered gone,
    is in my heart again.
I began smelling, touching, and feeling the

myriad flowers in the fields.
The spring air feels fresher and I am more alive
than ever.
I found my love; I found me!
"Who says that youthful love does not make a statement?"

Our parents have a powerful impact on how we grow and become adults; we have an impact on their lives. Mom was always there for me through thick and thin. Near the end of her life, when she was dying from cancer, she called and asked me to take her to the country for strawberries. I was more than happy to take this journey with Mom. This would be one of the richest days that I spent with my mother. It was my first trip to the strawberry fields and my favorite lady's last.

THE STAWBERRY FIELD IS LIFE

My mother asked me to drive her to the country
    where she and dad used to go annually
        to harvest strawberries.
Mom was fighting a battle with cancer and could not
    move around very well.
I picked her up one early summer morning and we
    drove leisurely to her favorite place,
        the strawberry field.
Betty wanted to harvest some of the berries for jams,
    pies, ice cream, and cereal.
The two of us drove slowly and enjoyed
    the country scenery.
Soon we arrived at the red colored fields where others
    were in the process of harvesting their
        treasured berries.
As I glanced at the fields, the rows of berries appeared
    to go on forever.
The countless rows bent, twisted, and were full of ripe
    berries for me to pluck with my hands.
Upon stopping the car, mother asked me if she could go
    use the portable toilet sitting quietly by the
        patches of strawberries.
Mom scarcely walked, as she was fighting for her life
    with terminal cancer.
The big C was daily taking a daily toll on her physical being;
Mom was wearing a diaper to help her with control concerning the
    bathroom.

Watching Mom fight to control her physical functions
        was not a fun thing for me to observe.
I was now the parent and Mom was the child.
Life has its distinct faces of ambiguities,
        metaphors, and paradoxes!
Mother groped my arm as I escorted her
        through the ruts and hedges to
                the "potty."
Mom always possessed determination, this was
        evident today; as we approached
                the portal of the bathroom,
                        she wanted to walk
                                the rest of the way herself.
Independence and grit are two faces Mom had
        as a parent.
Pulling the door open with her paltry energy,
        she entered the potty and shut the door.
As she closes the door, I waited outside crying.
After waiting for several minutes, Mother
        yelled that she needed help pulling her pants up.
I opened the door and went partway into the toilet;
I tugged on her drooping pants and pulled them up
        to her waist.
As I helpd Mom out of the outhouse, we both
        smiled as we celebrated our joint victory
                of her going to the bathroom.
I had a feeling of pride assisting my mother;
Mom helped me so many ways over
        my lifetime; she was my coach
                and mentor in so many ways!
As we walked back to the car, Mom yelled out, "I did it."
It was like she conquered running up a steep mountain peak;
In fact, she probably did.
I gave a ginger smile and hugged her like her little boy.
I had to go out in the field myself, as
        my mentor could not go with me.
The backbreaking bending and picking was too much
        work; I would do that myself.

Stoically, from the car, Mom watched
      me perform the task of picking the gems.
It was like she has a box seat viewing her son
      playing the strawberry game of life!
I left the car's air conditioning on and headed
      to the rich fields of berries.
I knew Mom was in deep pain; it hurt me to know
      she was suffering from cancer.
The ironic thing -- Mother never once complained to
      me about the hurt she was experiencing.
Seizing an empty basket, I was ready for my field
      trip to the patch.
I walked up and down the rows, snatching the delicious
      berries as Mom was my cheerleader from the car.
She waved occasionally, letting me know she was doing fine.
I was her little boy on a mission; I selected the
      gigantic and succulent trophies for Mom.
She liked the ones that she would bite into and the juice
      flowed like lava from a volcano into her mouth.
Flashing back, there was a time when Ma and Dad
      were both in good health; they enjoyed
         doing the simple things in life.
Dad died several years before Mom encountered her
      cancer full-blown.
If there is such a thing as giving a trophy to someone
      for showing you how to die with dignity,
         Mother would get one.
I would inscribe on the trophy these words: "To a
      berry good Mom who showed me how to live life."
While driving to the strawberry patch, we had a deep fulfilling
      conversation about God and life.
I recall Mom pointing to the big puffy clouds
      that hung with ease on the tapestry
         of the baby blue skies.
She commented how beautiful the hues were,
      and the simple elements which made
         up the heavenly skies that day.

We chatted about nature and God; how both of us
 loved the Lord and believed in the Triune God.
Mom made the comment about how we take for granted
 the "tiny" things God created for us.
One of her favorite animals she noticed on our trip
 was a Red-Tailed Hawk zooming above our car.
She stated, "I wish humans possessed keen
 eyesight like that Hawk."
I nodded my head up and down in agreement;
The conversation was smooth, silent, and holy.
Today, nine years later, the last trip to the
 strawberry field with Mother is
 etched in my soul.
The faith my mother showed that day for Jesus Christ
 was glaring through her actions and our conversations.
Mother demonstrated to me that day her faith was strong
 and stable.
She illustrated to me that God was holding her hand
 as she was experiencing turmoil and pain.
Mom died in October, four months after our journey as mother
 and son to the "field of life."
I want to thank my mommy for
 showing me how to live and die.
You lived, Mother, with integrity, dignity, and determination;
 above all, you possessed a Christ-like grace.
Forever, Mother, you will be the core fruit of my life.
Thanks for picking me for your son out of all of the
 berries in the field of life.
Thanks for allowing me to ripen and become a man.
Thanks for your tender ear and listening
 to my countless fears, which never came true.
Yes, mother, strawberries are grand.
I would say they are the "fruit of life."
"May I have another strawberry, please?"

A HOT DAY TO TROT

Chicago was the marathon to run
    with thousands assembled in the
        blazing October sun.
As race time drew near, ten thousand cancelled
    their quest in running the twenty-six mile test.
We started the race with runner-like zest;
    all participants wanted to do their best.
As we loped our pace, water was to be the biggest
    challenge in the race.
At mile two, the water was already gone;
I was singing the blues about what went wrong.
Life has its twists and turns in all that we do;
Running a marathon I found this also to be true.
Scuttling along Chicago's streets, I was
    experiencing the dreaded October heat.
Perspiration dripped liked a river flowing down my chest
    as I went galloping toward mile twenty-six.
At mile six the liquids ran low;
I wondered if this would be true for the rest of
    the marathon show?
Gasping for air, I threw off my shirt;
    knowing this was to be a long day for sure!
The temperature and heat index continued
    to run high; as my spirits ran low
        and my mouth was dry.
I sauntered slowly to mile seven and then to eight;
Many entrants were stopping to end the race.
They were sick and left out to dry; medical aid
    was needed at their sides.
Reaching mile ten, I started to walk;
I knew my training might be for naught.
I glimpsed around and others were slowing
    down too; some were actually
        turning blue.

As I continued to run the race, no water or
        Gatorade helped my pace.
The feeling of just wanting to survive was
        my sensation; there was not much liquid
                at any of the stations.
At one location they were out of cups,
        I took an empty dirty one from
                the gutter to see what water
                        I could scoop up.
Finding water in the tub, I fought for the last drop.
Approaching mile thirteen, I heard sirens coming
        down the street.
The reverberations of emergency vehicles
        blared on and on...
I knew something went terribly wrong.
Galloping, walking, and running a little too...
I conjectured what went wrong with the
        water supply and making runners blue.
Marathoners were dropping like flies from
        the sky; runners keep running with a sigh.
At mile thirteen, the police squealed that the race
        was complete.
The sun and heat index were villains to the
        runners' defeat.
People were yelling, "What happened to the race?"
However, they kept meandering on at a steady pace.
Now one of the top races in the world
        was a disgrace.
More than ten thousand people ended their quest
        to achieve their individual success.
Those behind mile thirteen were left out in the rain;
They were forced to stop in their tracks with no success.
Months of training were washed down in defeat
        as hundreds of runners were beaten by the heat.
At mile twenty, the directors halted the race; they
        redirected the runners to another place.
Many were frustrated and continued to run,

despite the warnings that the race was done.
As we went on a new route, not the path of the race,
      we walked four miles at a steady pace.
Soon we crossed the finish line's door;
Fans stood and cheered like never before.
The temperature and humidity pounded
      our spirits down; but cheers raised our
            spirits, and we were glad we were done.
Crossing the finish line I was happy, but
      my heart was yet on decline;
I wanted to do better; but this outcome was fine.
Life, which is the greatest gift,
      was taken from not one person, but from all of us.
When a brother or sister runner dies on their quest,
it kills my spirit and the heck with the rest.
Concluding my story of this run, I ask one question
      to the director of the race.
"When the Earth is three-fourths water and one-fourth land,
      how could you not deal the thousands
            of runners a winning hand...water!

CHAPTER SEVEN
LETTERS FROM FORMER STUDENTS

With humility and humbleness I share some of the letters that my former students have sent to me over the years. Like most teachers, I did not become abundantly rich with money by selecting a teaching career. Unlike businessmen and women, attorneys, physicians, and others that make thousands of dollars, teachers end up spending money and time dealing with their passion. I am blessed to have been called into the teaching profession; I am extremely wealthy in love and friendship that no one can put a price tag on.

Reflecting back on my life, I was not supposed to go to college and experience any success. My ADHD was undiagnosed for fifty years; the challenges in my life at times were overwhelming. I proudly shared my life story to show that no matter what others think or what obstacles there may be, you can rise to the bar of excellence in your own creative and loving ways. ADHD needs to be viewed as a gift, and not a weakness -- it is not a negative disorder! We simply must work on our weaknesses and traits.

Who would think that students would be writing to a person who flunked first grade, was thought to be mentally retarded, was at the bottom of his high school class, and flunked out of college once!

In the letters, I did not include the students' names; I have selected to share some of the letters from around the three hundred that I have received from students. At a later date, I hope to publish many of the notes I received.

Much of the correspondence came from end-of-the-year letters that students wrote to teachers who made an impact in the classroom -- *You Make a Difference* letters. They were written when I taught middle school for over a decade. Other correspondence simply came through the mail, computers, and during the school years that I taught elementary school.

TO: Mr. Weckerly

Thank you for teaching me, we all have talents; bringing new light to history made learning fun. I just got done taking the last quiz of the year in your class and I found it to be quite funny! Your wife sounds like she is almost as neat as you!

TO: Mr. Weckerly

Thank you for everything; this year was my best year of social studies. You were very convincing and nice; I especially like the History Alive curriculum. That opened up my feelings and helped me to express myself. You are a very good history teacher; thanks for making me have a good year. Thanks so very much.

Dear Mr. Weckerly,

As you read this letter, you probably will be in a state of utter confusion. I am a former student of yours. You were my sixth grade teacher at Marsh Elementary. I was a part of the first class that you taught in 1992. I do not expect you to remember me because the last time I saw you was the year after I left Marsh. My family and I moved to Tampa, in the middle of the year when I was in eighth grade. I am still residing here today.

The letter is more of a thank you note than anything else. With the exception of my senior year in high school, the sixth grade proved to be the greatest year of school for myself. One reason for this is memorable experiences. I think being teachers of a new school played a large part in this. Nevertheless, the main reason that sixth grade was so special to me was having you as a teacher. You have been one teacher who has influenced me more than anyone else throughout my primary education. For example, you taught me the correct structure for writing a three-part essay. Although my ideas and creativity might not have been so spectacular, the foundation and structure I used were always enough to get me the grade I wanted. You taught me more about poetry than all my teachers combined. You even took time out to teach us how to write poetry (I give you an extra big thanks for that because there is nothing a girl likes better than a good poem about her). You introduced me to many poets such as Langston Hughes and Robert Frost.

For my freshman year in English, I wrote a research paper on "choices of life," and how Robert Frost shows this in his poem the *Road Not Taken* and *Stopping by the Woods on a Snowy Evening.*" Believe it or not, I still have my poetry folder from sixth grade. I also remember the great amount of fun we had in your class. My mom still talks about the Halloween party we had. By the way, my mom adores you. You were the only teacher I know who had a mini basketball hoop in the classroom. I had other teachers who would teach with passion, but you are the only one who cared for each student. You would put us above any lesson plan if needed. I vividly remember the motto you used in our class. The quote read, "You are all unique and special." I still have the pencil you gave us that quote on! Thank you for giving me so much in just one year as a teacher.

Dear Mr. Weckerly,

Thanks Mr. Weckerly for opening my eyes to the world of poetry and social studies! I will always remember you as the teacher who "turned the tables on learning." Thank you for being a friend "who trotted down the road and back again." Oh, when I'm a millionaire, I'll buy you your cabin in the woods! Thank you so much. I hope our paths will cross again.

Dear Mr. Weckerly, (dated 4/10/2003)

I found the Eisenhower website online and it had an email address for you, so I hope this really is your email address. I had you as a US History teacher in 8th grade about six years ago. You probably won't remember me, but you had the greatest impact on my life. Right now, I am a freshman at the University of Illinois studying history in hopes of becoming an American History teacher. I chose history because between your class in 8th grade and my American History class in my junior year of high school, I found that history can be a very exciting topic that can help teach students not only about the past, but can also help them to understand the present and the future! I hope that I will be able to engage students in learning as you certainly did. I remember every detail of the conquests of Cortez from the trial you had us do on him (prosecuting).

You truly were an inspiring as a teacher and you made each student feel that they were an important part of the classroom!

Dear Mr. Weckerly,

I want to thank you for inspiring all of us to do our best; your constant optimism made everyone want to do better in class. You are as much as a teacher as a cheerleader.

Dear Mr. Weckerly, (1997-1998)

Thanks for having such a big impact on my life and education! It's hard to put into words how much respect I have for you as a person and teacher. You are one of the only teachers that treated me like an adult and not a fourteen-year-old eighth grader. After this year, I feel I have more confidence to stand up for myself and be my own person. I feel that I owe it all to you; thank you sooo much and I will miss you when I go to Guilford; you are the best!

Dear Mr. Weckerly, (1/21/07)

I sincerely hope that you do not mind receiving an email from a very grateful former student. I also hope that your daughter, Ginni, has told you of my meeting with her at Rockford College last Friday. After noting her first name is spelled as the same as mine, I recognized her last name!

First, I must tell you that you hold an extremely special place in my heart. Although I love my father very much, I had rather a difficult childhood; you were responsible for helping me find a straight path, one filled with enough confidence to push me forward and possess integrity. The beauty of your help, it was not forced; rather you gently encouraged me when I discovered the right paths, making me realize how truly good it was to have goals, dreams, and ideals. Thank you for your help, Mr. "W."

Mr. Weckerly, (1997-1998)

Well, well, this year sure has gone by fast, you have given so much!

You have taught me how to appreciate who I am and that no one is perfect! I wish you the best with your wife, poetry, your career, and life! I hope you stay in teaching for a long time because you are good at it. Well, thanks again! I love you! In a teacher and student way! Remember, "Tomorrow is but an illusion, all we have is today."

Dear Mr. "W," (class of 2001)

Thanks for helping through the last quarter in your class. You believed in me and knew I could do a lot more than I thought I could. It has been an honor to be in your class and have you for a teacher. It was very fun and educational at the same time. To tell you the truth, you are not like any other teacher I met. You are unique and that's a good thing because many teachers are not like that. It rubs off on the student and they think "outside of the box."

Dear Mr. Weckerly,

I want to thank you for always pushing me to do my best and not giving up on me when I wasn't doing well. I will never forget the different styles of note taking you taught me. Words don't explain how grateful I am.

Dear Mr. Weckerly,

Thanks for teaching me about history this year; I learned a lot in your class. Also, thanks for going to Washington D.C. with us. I really enjoyed being on your bus and talking with you. You really have many interesting things to say. I really liked your poetry too. I write a lot of poetry, but not many people know about it. I have had some poems published. That was cool I think. You made this year fun for me. Thank you very much.

P.S. I hope to keep in touch in the future.

Dear Mr. "W,"

I want you to know that you taught me more than just history; you taught me that it is ok to fail (as long as you learn from it). Maybe you did not know, but you helped me through problems by just giving advice that you gave in class. You taught me that a good thinker makes many choices available in problem solving.

The gift I gave to you has special meaning. The smiley face thing stands for all the things you have talked about, like when you fall, pick yourself up and move on. The pencils stand for the few that I borrowed from you and you always said to never give them away. The picture is of my greatest achievement when I won second place in Sweden. You said something about giving away something that you value the most to others. That way, you truly are experiencing love and success. The silver medal I won I will keep for a while.

Dear Mr. Weckerly, (June 2001)

Once upon a time, a girl loved to write; she would write stories, poems, and songs or anything she could think of. She was quite good actually, but not many people took notice of her writings. Than one year, when she was thirteen years old, she met a friend, who was a teacher. The girl's new friend was also a writer, and he was kind and caring toward her.

Well, the year went by, and it was time for the girl to move to a new school. She'd no longer see her cherished friend five days a week. But forever, she'd keep in mind the kindness her friend had shown her. She will remember him always; her 8th grade U.S. History teacher in 6th hour, her friend.

Mr. Weckerly,

I wanna thank you for making a difference in my life. You always believed in me, that I could bring my grades up. I did! I liked how we did the SQ3R Reading Method and mind maps. I enjoyed giving oral reports from them. The plays we did about history events were fun and educational.

Thank you for having confidence in me!

Dear Mr. Weckerly,

You are one of my favorite teachers; learning in your class was lots of fun. When you're ready to take guitar lessons, let me know, just kidding, unless you really would like to. Well, it has been a blast in your class. Thanks again. You are great.

Dear Mr. Weckerly,

Hello! I decided to write you a happy note because I understand that you are going through a rough time in your life. No matter how much you yell at me and our 7th hour class, I would like you to know I will never think less of you. You've given me so much knowledge about history and life. Not to mention a pen and paper which I am writing on. I got them from you! So to sum up this note, it is my way of saying, "Thank you for being one of the best educators I had the privilege of knowing. See you in seventh hour."

P.S.: "Great people, with enormous hearts, only come around once in a while, thanks for being one of those people!"

Dear Mr. "W,"

I liked it when you showed and shared your poetry with us. You not only told us about love, kindness, and friendship, but you lived it. You made me see not the bad side of the world all the time, but the good part of the world. Thanks for all of the compliments you gave me. They made me feel good. Another thing, thanks for helping me understand things that I could not get. I really appreciated all that you have done.

Dear Mr. Weckerly,

Thanks for being such a good and crazy teacher! Not only did you teach us about U.S. History, but also how to control our anger through your lectures. I really hope my cousin gets you for a teacher next year. He could learn more from you about himself. My little brother could learn how to raise his self-esteem too. He is very scared to try something new. You can teach him that failure is not bad, and trying to have fun learning even though you do not get everything correct. Also, since I am in the Rockford Ski Broncos, I want to thank you; I was scared to try out, however, you encouraged me to do so and I made the team!

EPILOGUE

I live a good life and many people have helped me to transform my life into something meaningful. I want to thank God for allowing the loving and not so loving people into my life to teach me what the journey of life is all about.

Living in the 1950s and 1960s was a wonderful experience; I never have wished that I lived in other eras. Every day was magical and mystical as far as living life. The events which happened while I was growing up forged my attitudes and way of living.

Not knowing that I had ADHD for fifty years was painful, as it was, and yet still is, for us boomers who never knew that such a thing as ADHD existed. However, learning at age fifty that I had the disorders and traits enlightened me about why I behaved the way I did.

I now look at ADHD as a gift; it does have its flip side, however. By embracing my strong points and trying to strengthen the weak ones, I have become a better human.

I toast and lift a glass of faith to those who will take a sincere look at where they are personally and have the desire to change. Swallow that drink of faith and know that there is light at the end of the tunnel. Your life!

REFERENCES/RESOURCES

www.focusonadhd.com
www.Webmd.com
www.wrongdiagnosis.com
ADHD.TreatmentsInfo.com
www.addadhdblog.com
www.help4adhd.org
www.adhdsupport.com
www.healthcentral.com
www.healthcentral.com
www.symptomfind.com
GetADHDTreatments.com
Www.Healthline.com
Adaa.org
www.upliftprogram.com
www.DiseaseLinked.com
www.Adult-ADHD-success.com
ezinearticles.com
www.additudemag.com
www.eveningpsychiatrist.com
www.health.wa.gov.au
www.symptomfind.com
addtestonline.com
www.add.adhdnews.com
news.healingwell.com
www.addresources.org
ADHD.3StepsADD.com
AdhdHub.net

ADHD (ADD) HELPING ORGANIZATIONS

Attention Deficit Disorder Association (ADDA)
P.O. Box 543, Pottstown, PA 19464
484-945-2101

Children and Adults with Attention Deficit Disorder (CHADD)
8181 Professional Place, Suite 150, Landover MD 20785
301-3067070
www.chadd.org
CHADD is involved in scientific research and public education.
CHADD works to help those who have ADHD reach their potential in all phases of life.

LEARNING

www. add.org
This is the clearinghouse nationally for information, advocacy and support for ADHD adults.

Council for Learning Disabilities
P.O. Box 4014, Leesburg, Va 20177
571-258-1010
www.cldinternational.org
This is an international organization which focuses on problems related to students who have learning disabilities.

Educational Resources Information Center (ERIC)
2277 Research Boulevard, 6M, Rockville, MD 20850
301-519-5157, 800-538-3742
www.eric.ed.gove; email: eric@ericit.syr.edu
This is funded by the United States Department of Education.
ERIC is a national information system dedicated to helping people with learning disabilities.

National Institute for Learning Disabilities
107 Seekel Street, Norfolk, VA 23505
757-423-8646
www.nild.net
This institute developed its own unique education and therapy plan for individuals with ADD/LD. The organization tutors, using educational exercises that stimulate the brain.

COACHING RESOURCES

ADD Coach Register
www.add.org
This provides a list of ADD coaches in the United States.

American Coaching Association
P.O. Box 353 Lafayette Hill, PA 19144
610-825-8572
www.americoach.org
This organization trains coaches and helps people to become familiar with coaching and what it is all about.

READINGS FOR ADULT ADDERS

Amen, Daniel G., M.D. *Healing ADD (Putnam, 2001).*
　　Dr. Amen talks about his six classifications of ADHD (ADD) and provides an all inclusive treatment program that can help ADDers lead a constructive and full life. He offers a test to see with which of the six categories an individual may identified.

Flick, Grad L., Ph.D., *ADD/ADHD Behavior –Change Resource Kit (Jossey-Ross1998).*
　　Dr. Flick provides ready-to-use strategies and activities for children with ADHD. I highly recommend this for adults with ADHD. Also, there are some great ideas you can incorporate into your life.

Goleman, Daniel, *Social Intelligence (Bantam Dell, 2006).*

ADDers are highly intuitive and can have the ability to get along with many types of people. The ways we interact with others have the power to shape our brains. Goleman states that our brains are hardwired to connect to others and can use our kindness to make the world a better place.

Hallowell, Edward M., M.D., *Worry (1997).*

ADDers are people who worry. Although this book applies to all people, this is great for adult ADDers. Dr. Hallowell states, "While a healthy level of worry can help us perform efficiently at work, anticipate dangers, and learn from past errors, in its extreme forms worry can become "toxic"-poisoning our pleasures, sabotaging our achievements, and preventing us from resolving actual problems."

Hallowell, Edward M., and John J. Ratey, M.D., *Driven to Distraction: Getting the Most Out of Life with Attention Deficit Disorder (Ballantine Books, 2006).*

This book addresses ADD learning styles and attention spans--a must read for all people with ADHD!

Hartman, Thomas, *Attention Deficit Disorder: A Different Perception* (Underwood Books, 1997).

Mr. Hartman explains many of the positive attributes that are associated with ADD and explains the disorder of ADHD. He talks about how ADD adults can deal with their problems at home, in school, or at work.

Kelly, Kate, and Peggy Ramundo, *You Mean I'm Not Lazy, Stupid, or Crazy?!* (Scribner, 1996).

Both authors have ADD. This book offers adults with ADHD a guide in dealing with their disorder. The book concentrates on the experiences of adults with ADHD and offers updated information in research and suggests how to move forward with ADHD coaching.

Kolberg, Judith, and Kathleen Nadeau, Ph.D., *ADD –Friendly Ways to Organize Your Life (Brunner-Routledge, 2002).*
The authors talk about organizing your life and offer excellent suggestions on how to progress ahead in dealing with disorganization issues.

CPSIA information can be obtained at www.ICGtesting.com
Printed in the USA
LVOW06s0833050314

375888LV00003B/275/P